TODAY IS NOT LIKE YESTERDAY

TODAY IS NOT LIKE YESTERDAY

A Chilean Journey

photographs by Ted Polumbaum
text by Nyna Brael Polumbaum

LIGHT & SHADOW

CAMBRIDGE, MASSACHUSETTS

Book design by Nyna Brael Polumbaum. Printed in Singapore. Copyright © 1992 by Ted Polumbaum and Nyna Brael Polumbaum. First edition.
Library of Congress Catalog Card Number: 92-072568   ISBN 0-9633526-0-1

Today is not like yesterday
That is certain, brother
We have become old waiting for the roses
to return and fill the air with their luminosity,
but the great wave will come over us
and with each blow to the rocks
new seeds will be born
to build the house.

Ramón Riquelme,
written in prison

Published by LIGHT & SHADOW, One Kendall Square, Suite 2200, Cambridge, MA 02139. Tel: (617) 621-7059 Fax: (617) 491-4948

The Chile we remember, a poor and isolated land of dreams and desperation, has become an outstanding success in the international marketplace. Its kiwis and grapes spill from northern supermarket counters in winter, its fish are ground into meal and shipped far away, its forests hammered into houses in Australia and Japan. Today's Chile, smug and stylish, seems like any other little country, and our passion for it may at last be spent. We hope our friends there will forgive us for indulging in the nostalgia which they have had to put aside as they struggle to survive the New World Order.

Chile—that lean strand between the Andes and the Pacific, with so many landscapes and climates, from sun-scorched rainless north through fertile vineyards of the central valley, Andean peaks and towering pines, to the wet, sub-arctic south. Famous for Darwin's voyage and two islands, one where Robinson Crusoe was mythically cast ashore, the other the site of mysterious volcanic heads that might have been scattered by gods. The home of two poets—a man and a woman—each of whom won the Nobel Prize for literature. Those things are all true.

Chile—also famous for its civility and restraint, for an abiding constitutional tradition and the respect of its military for constitutional rule. Those things turned out to be false.

Our fondness for the Chileans and our obsession with the country's sad fate continued for so long that when we were there recently, searching for people we had known, a man who saw Ted through a doorway but failed to recognize Nyna exclaimed, "Hey! I know you. Whatever happened to the young woman who was with you the last time you were here?"

For us, it all started in 1970, with the election of Salvador Allende as president of Chile. The dapper doctor, whose family tree included Air Force Col. Marmaduke Grove, who had dropped leaflets from a little plane to proclaim the socialist republic that lasted twelve days in 1932, had run for the office three times before.

Ted spent only ten days there at the time of Allende's inaugural, but both of us returned for two longer visits during the brief years of the "Popular Unity." We found friends in shantytowns where gifted people were struggling, with some success, to create organized communities from the chaos of joblessness, homelessness, alcohol and prostitution. At nationalized factories we watched workers sitting on boards of directors, learning to run industries along with the experts. In the grim coal zone we met families whose militancy went back for generations. On farms they had seized we saw landless peasants turning over dirt they thought was finally their own. We also understood the seething resentment of the middle classes—people just like us—whose money was declining in value even as they lined-up for dwindling supplies of necessities, from chickens to toilet paper.

It was a time when nothing seemed impossible, no sacrifice too great. It was also a time of human failings, arrogance and bad luck. Indeed, Allende's coalition might have fallen from the weight of internecine squabbles or its own mistakes, but the Popular Unity never had a chance to stand or fall on its own. Allende believed it was possible to change the society while playing by the rules—within the bounds of the existing constitution, existing judicial system, even the existing military apparatus— while retaining full freedom for the press, and parties of the opposition. That was a chimera.

The experiment was doomed from the beginning; in the end a venomous domestic opposition abandoned its pretensions to gentility and pluralism and cheered the bloody coup that brought General Augusto Pinochet to power.

Almost a generation later we returned to witness the victory of Patricio Aylwin, the candidate of the democratic opposition, over Pinochet's hand-picked choice for president. Exiles were still coming home from the far-off places to which they had fled after the coup. The families of the disappeared kept searching for corpses, which were still being found after all these years—in a remote grave, an abandoned shaft, a morgue refrigerator or mummified by the desert.

Surprisingly, the survivors of torture and the relatives of the missing do not seek vengeance or expect justice, but they do demand truth. A well-documented report by the government-appointed Commission of Truth and Reconciliation has brought some of that truth to light. Some members of the military, and their supporters, assert that the supposed atrocities are a hoax, and the "disappeared" are simply enjoying extended vacations abroad. Others acknowledge that abuses took place and express regret, but see them as a reasonable price to have paid for the ensuing prosperity. Despite the return to democracy, truth remains an elusive and contested goal.

This is our version of what happened in Chile, arrived at in the course of a search through city, small town and countryside for people we had known before blacklisting, prison, torture, exile and murder scattered them through their own country and to strange lands. We offer you sagas of these ordinary people—then and now—who tried mightily to change their world and paid dearly for their audacity.

Nyna Brael Polumbaum & Ted Polumbaum
Cambridge, Massachusetts, May 1992

1541 Pedro de Valdivia marches from Peru, settles Santiago and meets fierce resistance from the indigenous Araucanos in the south.

1552 Lautaro, once Valdivia's page, leads Araucanos in battles against the Spanish. Valdivia is killed. Insurrections recur for three centuries.

1810 September 18th, still a national holiday, marks Chilean independence from Spain.

1817 "Great Liberator" Bernardo O'Higgins becomes Chile's first head of state. He ends his life in voluntary exile.

1831 Darwin sets out on the six year-long voyage of the Beagle.

1833 The first Chilean constitution establishes elections of president and parliament.

1879–1882 In the War of the Pacific, Chile wins the vast copper and nitrate wealth of the Atacama desert from Peru and cuts off Bolivia's access to the sea. Actual mine ownership remains mainly in British hands.

1906 Valparaíso, Chile's Pacific port, is destroyed by earthquake and firestorm. Printer Luis Emilio Recabarren is elected to Parliament.

1907 Government troops fire on nitrate miners who gather in the desert port of Iquique to protest brutal working conditions. As many as two thousand are killed.

1911 Guggenheim acquires the world's largest open pit copper mine from the British. It is then sold to Anaconda in 1923.

1925 The Constitution of 1925 (remaining in effect until 1973 military coup) includes provisions for separation of Church and State, direct taxation and social welfare.

1932 Air Force Col. Marmaduke Grove proclaims a Socialist republic which is overthrown after twelve days.

1938 Native Nazis attempt a coup, but get little support.

1948 The "Law for the Defense of Democracy" is passed, the Communist Party is outlawed and many members sent to jail or internal exile. Senator Pablo Neruda, who later received the Nobel Prize for literature, is unseated.

1949 Women get the vote.

1952 Salvador Allende runs for president for the first time as the candidate of the Socialist party.

1953 The CUT (Central Workers Union) is founded.

1958 Allende runs for president a second time.

1964 Allende runs again but Christian Democrat Eduardo Frei wins, with the help of a $3 million campaign gift from the U.S.

1965 The MIR (Revolutionary Left Movement) is founded.

1969 A military uprising led by right-wing Gen. Roberto Viaux is put down by Frei. The U.P. (left-of-center Popular Unity) is formed. Kennecott Copper's rate of return on Chilean investment is 205% while its worldwide profit is 10%.

1970 U.P. candidate Allende wins presidential election over Christian Democrat Rodimiro Tomic and National Party's Jorge Alessandri, with 36.3% of the vote. Army Chief-of-Staff René Schneider is assassinated; Ex-Gen. Viaux is jailed. Congress ends uncertainty by ratifying Allende victory. General Augusto Pinochet appears by his side at inaugural celebrations.

1971 Copper is nationalized by unanimous vote of Congress.

1972 "The Secret Documents of ITT," based on revelations by American columnist Jack Anderson, is published in Chile. The best seller consists of photocopies of correspondence from ITT officers revealing schemes with the CIA and the "40" Committee, headed by Henry Kissinger, to subvert the election process and make Allende's government unworkable. Richard Nixon announces a hard line policy. Allende addresses U.N. on foreign intervention in his country. The U.S. disburses cash to finance a 26-day truck owner's strike which paralyzes the country's distribution system, and funnels money to fascist "Fatherland and Liberty" group.

1971–1973 An "invisible blockade" strangles U.P. government. Export-Import Bank loans go from $600 million total to zero; US commercial credit from $300 million under Frei to $30 million; Inter-American Development Bank loans from $46 million to $2 million; World Bank loans from $234 million total to zero. Washington continues aid to the military for weapons, counter-insurgency training and parties and trips to the U.S. for officers; also to American Institute for Free Labor Development for infiltrating unions.

1972–1973 The period is marked by increasing opposition stridency, government blunders, uncontrolled peasant land seizures, high inflation, lack of spare parts for foreign-made machinery, shortages of goods and food, hoarding, capital flight and growing power of the military.

1973 June 29th abortive coup is probably a dress rehearsal for real coup. Chief-of-Staff Gen. Carlos Prats, supporter of constitutional rule, is hounded from his post. He and his wife are later assassinated in Buenos Aires. The presidential palace is bombed and the military overthrows the elected government on September 11th. Allende commits suicide. High officials are banished to a bleak Antarctic island. A three-man military junta begins 17 years of dictatorship. Americans Charles Horman and Frank Teruggi are murdered but the U.S. embassy impedes an investigation and discovery of the bodies (subject of film "Missing"). Pablo Neruda dies and hundreds of people, including the Swedish ambassador and heads of the Christian Democratic Party and Catholic University, defy a prohibition on gatherings to attend his funeral. The ruling junta takes over universities, suspends political parties and trade unions, revokes citizenship of political opponents.

1974 Pinochet demotes his junta partners and becomes sole dictator.

1975 U.S. Senate Intelligence Committee hearings reveal the shocking extent of American intervention in Chile. Economist Milton Friedman and his "Chicago Boys" are invited there to begin "shock treatment" to control raging inflation and privatize the economy.

1976 On a Washington, D.C. street, ex-ambassador to the U.S. Orlando Letelier and American colleague Ronni Moffit are assassinated by a remote control car bomb. The Carter administration cools relations when Chile refuses to cooperate. Bombing planner Michael Townley pleads guilty and talks, implicating two anti-Castro Cubans.

1981 The Chilean economic miracle grows, then deflates as banks go into crisis and collapse. Pinochet intervenes to bail out scandal-ridden banks. Chile, owing $21 billion, becomes the world's most indebted nation, per capita. U.S. Ambassador to the U.N. Jeanne Kirkpatrick praises Pinochet.

1983 May 11th marks the first big public protests against the dictatorship. An opposition press surfaces.

1986 Young Chilean Carmen Gloria Quintana and Washington, D.C. resident Rodrigo Rojas, an exile's son, are doused with kerosene by soldiers and set afire. He dies after two days. Badly burned, she survives. The Manuel Rodriguez Patriotic Front attacks Pinochet's motorcade as it approaches Santiago from his vacation home. Pinochet escapes unscathed when two shells which make direct hits on his car misfire, but guards are killed. Repression increases.

1987 Repression eases for a Papal visit. Pope John Paul II embraces the disfigured Carmen Gloria.

1988 The October plebiscite, designed to legitimize a Pinochet presidency backfires when 92% of eligible voters vote 43.04% YES to 54.68% NO. Now Pinochet cannot become president.

1989 The first presidential election in 19 years is on December 14th. Pinochet's candidate Hernán Büchi and self-made businessman Francisco Errázuriz are soundly defeated by 71 year-old Christian Democrat Patricio Aylwin, candidate of the unified center-left opposition. A bellicose Pinochet still controls the Army.

1990 Exiles continue to return. Aylwin appoints 80 year-old jurist Raul Rettig to head a nine-person commission to investigate violations of human rights. Even after incontrovertible evidence, punishment is unlikely because Pinochet had declared an amnesty for crimes between 1973 and 1978, when the greatest number of atrocities were committed.

1991 The five-volume report of the Commission of Truth and Reconciliation, documenting some 2500 deaths and disappearances, shocks the nation, but coverage of the Rettig report is soon supplanted by headlines about terrorism. The popular head of a right wing party is assassinated after publicly insulting Gen. Manuel Contreras, ex-head of the secret police. In the U.S. another Cuban is arrested in the Letelier-Moffit killings as a result of an "America's Most Wanted" television broadcast. In Chile, only days before the statute of limitations runs out, Justice Bañados orders the arrest of Gen. Contreras and his operations chief Col. Pedro Espinoza for the same crime. Digging commences in a pauper's section of the Santiago General Cemetery and scores of tortured, bullet-ridden corpses, some of them children, are disinterred. Pinochet quips that doubled-up corpses found in some graves show sound economics.

1992 An international arbitration panel orders the Chilean government to pay $2.5 million in reparations to the families of Letelier and Moffit.

Salvador Allende had always accepted defeat with grace. His opponents were not so civil. Three years after Allende became president, having governed for only half his allotted time, the military bombed and invaded the presidential palace, inside which he then killed himself. They filled stadiums with prisoners, burned books, applied electric current to flesh, and made people disappear. Thousands fled or were expelled from the country. The killings even continued abroad: an ex-general in Buenos Aires and an ex-ambassador in Washington were assassinated; an ex-political leader was maimed in Rome.

A generation of children grew up in a dark time and their parents remained silent and afraid. The poor went hungry much of the time while the rich became very rich. Everybody could see how much General Pinochet had done for the poor because the men who lay prone in the public parks, cutting grass with hand shears until it was like velvet, had been costumed in bright orange coveralls. Their salaries under the general's program served only to help the children starve more slowly.

When the children grew a little older they became more angry than afraid. They threw rocks, set up barricades, and were knocked down by water cannon on the streets. The mothers of the disappeared still searched for their sons and daughters, while church human rights workers offered the widows and orphans soup and hope. Many of the "better" people began to distance themselves from the crude general they had once welcomed. Still, they said, the victims had brought hardship on themselves by fomenting class hatred.

After sixteen years Pinochet, who wanted the people to prove they loved him, ordered a plebiscite in which they must vote, "YES! We want you to be not only our dictator, but our president." But when the ballots were counted, it turned out that in their secret cubicles the people had said "NO!" Everybody stopped being afraid and came out in the streets to dance. True joy, however, did not return so easily.

The new president, an avowed socialist who had once missed being elected by 3% and was defeated another time by an infusion of three million U.S. dollars to his rival, used to quip that his tombstone would read, "Here lies Salvador Allende, future president of Chile."

When he ran for a fourth time in 1970, the red cover of Time magazine blazed, "Marxist Threat in the Americas." The story warned, "If he is denied the presidency, his followers may well plunge the country into a murderous civil war. But if he is acknowledged the winner . . . Chile may not have another free election for a very long time."

"U.S. Yawns at Chile Vote," the New York Times initially observed. "Some people are interested, but the last thing anyone thinks of is doing something about it." In fact, the United States did try.

Allende's opponents frightened voters with a nightmare scenario if they chose him. Advertisements showed tanks rolling and barbed wire festooning a street "where children once played." A photograph of a dejected mother and son bore the caption, "Where is his father? Torn from home, found in prisons, concentration camps or disappeared, just for differing with the government."

All those things happened. The surprise was that those who later betrayed democracy were the very same people who had warned most vociferously that Allende would destroy Chile's traditional freedoms.

right: November 6, 1970. Allende rides through cheering crowds in an open car after being sworn-in. The atmos–phere is tense. His victory in a three-way race with only 36.3% of the vote spawned outrage and intrigue by the Chilean right-wing, a rogue general, high ITT officials, current and former heads of the CIA and Henry Kiss-inger. Plots were hatched to deny him the presidency, including one to bribe the Chilean congress. Allende (center) is guarded by three groups: uniformed Carab-ineros (national police), plainclothes detectives from the unpopular "Investigations" and young men of the GAP (Group of Personal Friends), who take on his defense because they do not trust the others. (Many GAP members were executed in the early hours of the 1973 coup.)

above: October 1970. Worried throngs gather outside a hospital on the route of the funeral cortege of assassinated Army chief René Schneider. Zealots led by ex-Gen. Roberto Viaux—who had been cashiered by President Eduardo Frei for attempting a coup—plotted with CIA operatives carrying dollars and weapons to keep Allende from assuming office. Henry Kissinger later claimed that the U.S. had withdrawn its support before Schneider was mortally wounded in an attack on his car.

right: Allende and outgoing Pres. Frei at Gen. Schneider's funeral.

right: 1970. On the walls of a village school, official portraits of heads of state from "Great Liberator" Bernardo O'Higgins to Eduardo Frei are displayed. The original presidential sash, handed down through centuries, was destroyed in the military era. For the 1989 inaugural of Patricio Aylwin, Chile's first elected president in nearly 20 years, a replica had to be created.

right: Santiago, 1972. During the three years of the Popular Unity, it seemed that artists, graffiti artists and students were trying to cover every blank wall in the country. Muralists worked in teams: one to sketch, a second with yellow brush, a third to paint flesh tones, then blue, red and so on, until every shape was filled. Last came the black outlines. Panels for this mural, extending hundreds of feet around the square adjoining the presidential palace, began going up at three one afternoon. Four hours after a brigade swarmed over the surface with paint and brushes, the president mounted the platform at the center of the finished mural to address the nation on television. By morning the square was empty again. The day after the military takeover murals throughout the nation were obliterated.

above: 1970. Bored with politics, high school students in an affluent Santiago suburb, hang out near the "Drugstore." After school they shed their uniforms, put on jeans and imitate what they think is the U.S. lifestyle.

right: Santiago, 1970. Politically active university students march along in the inaugural celebration.

above: Santiago, 1972. Middle class women of the opposition come out to protest shortages and long lines with the slogan, "No to the Communist Yoke." (This demonstration was the only occasion in five visits to Chile on which the writer and photographer were threatened with harm. Club-wielding members of "Fatherland and Liberty" backed off when we indignantly flashed U.S. press credentials.)

right: Santiago, 1972. Shantytown women ridicule the complaints of affluent women. Their placard offers pots of food and commands, "Eat, Mummy Bigmouth!" Mummy was a favorite epithet for conservatives.

Life and Death of a Shantytown

Shantytowns that sprang up overnight on the fringes of the cities were called "callampas" (fungi), and the displaced slum dwellers and rural migrants who swarmed onto empty lots at night with their babies and meager possessions were known as "rotos" (broken or ragged ones). Their miserable shacks were without water, without power, without municipal services. The floors were dirt and the roofs—of corrugated metal, tar paper or wood scraps held down by rocks, bald tires and refuse—leaked when it rained and collapsed when it snowed. Dust swirled in the air all summer and mud oozed underfoot all winter.

The addition of primitive amenities made life a little easier: a single water tap shared by hundreds of families, a few watts of electricity stolen from the nearby pole, a rosebush in a tin can. Still, the garbage piled up, the ramshackle privies stank and infant dysentery was endemic. Except for stalls where bagged food and cigarettes were sold, shops were far away. The bus seldom passed, and there were no doctors, no schools, no movie houses or churches.

Life was chaotic and violent. By the age of ten, children dropped out of school to roam the neighborhood in packs. Many of the working men were unskilled laborers or street vendors, and among the unemployed there was drunkenness, wife-beating and prostitution. Rotos existed on the margins, outside the economy, excluded from the political process.

By the 1960s, shantytown squatters had come to be viewed as a festering, threatening force. Reformers took notice. Eduardo Frei's Christian Democratic government (1964–1970) set up mothers' centers and neighborhood councils in existing shantytowns. They designated large tracts for future planned development, but as soon as lots were marked off on the elaborate site maps, families rushed in to lay claims by throwing together shanties. Church workers soon came knocking to provide services, quickly followed by social scientists conducting studies.

By the end of the decade these urban homesteaders had become the first mass constituency of the Revolutionary Left Movement (MIR), formed in the universities by children of privilege who were impatient with the measured steps of traditional leftist parties. As the Frei administration wound down, residents were preparing to fuse three separate shantytowns led by the MIR into one vast encampment they would call New Havana. The camp came to life at almost the same moment Allende's government took office. It lasted as an organized community until the 1973 military coup which ended that government.

Through a series of threats, militant demonstrations and takeovers the shantytown dwellers acquired 212 acres of farmland southeast of Santiago. They employed similar confrontational tactics to get technical assistance and help with their master plan, including the dumping of a mini-shantytown on the doorstep of the University of Chile School of Architecture. That resulted in an unlikely collaboration of professors and students from two universities, experts from government ministries, and stubborn, uneducated squatters who knew exactly what they wanted.

For the first phase, on the tenth of the land that had been set aside for temporary shelters, wide streets were staked out, equal sized lots marked off, water lines buried, and drainage ditches dug. The 1,300 families who moved en masse from their old hovels found a water tap at every corner, garbage enclosures and latrines on the perimeter of the camp, and tall stacks of prefabricated panels with which to begin building. The second phase, including clinic, mothers' center, dining hall, theater and nursery school, began rising only after the wheat which had been growing there was harvested for cash.

The final structures would be masonry houses for almost nine thousand residents, allocated by family size. The designs incorporated many proposals from the settlers, the most ingenious being an overhang as wide again as the house, inspired by Hollywood westerns. The architects sent back a memo of praise, but reduced the size of the cantilever to keep the houses from tipping over.

With government backing, the camp set up its own construction company. For many of the formerly unskilled unemployed, who comprised a third of the building crew, it became the first time they were learning a trade, punching a time clock, or receiving a regular pay envelope. To guarantee that the remarkable spirit of cooperation which developed around the house-building would not be lost, it was decided that no single family would occupy its new home until every single one was finished.

The camp's elaborate governing structure was a pyramid, with a five-person, elected council at the top and a General Assembly—open to all and meeting outdoors in the evening—at the bottom. In between, the basic unit was the block, each occupied by 64 families on identical 16'×25' sites. Each block elected officers and also sent delegates to a 25-person directorate and eight working committees known as fronts.

The Health Front managed the clinics, an ambulance, and sanitation, including latrine-cleaning and anti-fly propaganda. The Cultural Front put out a newsletter and was in charge of the schools, adult literacy and theatre. The Vigilance Front, armed with leather truncheons, guarded the camp and meted out rough justice for drunkenness, wife-beating, fighting and petty crime. The Mother's Front proposed a dining hall to liberate women from cooking in their primitive kitchens and took care of sick children in a warm room. Green Front members planted trees on weekends and planned a future Avenue of Oranges and Lemons.

The settlers craved nothing so much as decent homes and easier lives, while the leaders, including Mickey, New Havana's combative young chief, were determined to build "revolutionary consciousness."

The friendly Allende government provided construction materials. It sent doctors and nurses from the National Health Service to staff the clinics, and teachers to preside over ancient buses which had been refurbished as temporary classrooms. Even so, the leaders remained suspicious of reformers and continued their confrontational tactics.

Every decision, large or small, was argued vociferously. When a chain link fence went up around the schoolyard without debate, outraged cries of "authoritarian" and "concentration camp" arose from one faction, while more pragmatic people recognized that kids who had never before attended school might be tempted to run off when they became bored. The fence stayed.

The dusty streets were alive with wagons, children, and dogs. Posters were slapped onto every surface to warn of flies, tuberculosis and counter-revolution. Outside one house a man hammered copper sheets into sentimental scenes featuring Don Quixote, while two assistants, awkward in their mini-skirts, bent over to shine the finished plaques. A couple of masked men ground onyx into ash trays under a choking dust cloud and two women were visible through a window, one cutting the hair of a sheet-covered boy, the other turning shirt collars on a foot powered Singer.

Nobody objected to the presence of two observers from the north as we hovered at the edge of a General Assembly meeting, eavesdropped on the intense theorizing of the Cultural Front and watched a committee tally the camp census by candlelight. On a rainy winter afternoon we drank forbidden wine in a shack, wondering how many small children might have been burned by charcoal braziers like the one that provided the family's only heat. We watched two young women training to work in the clinic, and met another who handled the ambulance detail better than any man before her. After we asked one fellow how he planned to conduct the armed struggle he predicted the future would bring, he showed us his tiny .22 on a shelf.

The camp's legendary success brought a procession of curious foreigners: scholars, journalists, planners, sympathizers and self-styled revolutionaries. Some, like us, were observers, fascinated by the changes people were making in their own lives; some sought answers to the housing problems that plagued the third world; some sought adventure. Those who came with notebooks went back to their own comfortable quarters at night. A few of the adventurers moved in with the camp's best-looking single women.

Rock star Country Joe McDonald, one of the more glamorous U.S. visitors, had helped paint wall slogans before the election. "When he was painting with us a beautiful thing happened. We had to fight when we were attacked by cops and made our get-away by jumping over fences," one resident boasted.

The organization of the camp was so effective that for a week following the military coup and Allende's death, with helicopters circling overhead and gunfire all around, life went on without major disruption. Santiago was in chaos, but here the food distribution continued, building crews kept working to finish the houses, and many people still believed they would move into their new homes on the rapidly approaching target date.

Even after Mickey, the top leader, vanished into the MIR underground, hardly anyone comprehended the magnitude of the coup until soldiers began hauling people off to jail, and children on their way to school began finding the bodies of strangers on the street outside the camp. A few people were killed and one man went mad after torture. Entire families fled into exile. The military renamed the community "New Dawn," and moved outsiders into the new houses they had been building for themselves.

Two decades later, trees and scruffy gardens soften the appearance of the neighborhood, but the "temporary" shacks are still there, most of them still occupied by original settlers or their children. Some look more dilapidated than ever, though others have been improved by wood floors, additions, and strong iron fences.

Almost every family experienced under-employment or un-employment during the Pinochet years. Many were dependent on the soup kitchens run by the church. Private agencies now conduct pre-school programs for a small number of children in New Dawn and other slums, but social service workers are pessimistic about saving the children who are once again dropping out of school at an early age. Any parked car invites a break-in, muggings are common, and even the poorest families are afraid to leave their shabby homes unguarded.

Chile has become rich, but the poor, here and elsewhere, have been isolated, starved and terrorized. The idealism which once imbued community life, the services which helped keep their children healthy, the structures which held people together and gave them hope for a better life, have been decimated. The new government offers them hope for the future, but for now they are on their own again—just surviving.

above: Santiago outskirts, 1970. When squatters seized this land they brought along their children, and materials for crude shelters. In the past, police had often cordoned off intruders to keep them from establishing settlements, sometimes routing them with clubs. Beginning with the waning days of the Frei government, the treatment of squatters became more indulgent.

right: Santiago, 1970. Shantytown hovels, built of scrap, are cold and wet in winter, sweltering in summer. These washerwomen must carry pails of water from a distant tap to fill their wooden laundry tubs.

Soon after the coup Chile's leading newspaper, El Mercurio, which had long been supported by U.S. dollars, turned its front page into a wanted poster on behalf of Chile's military rulers. "**The Governing Military Junta Orders: LOCATE AND ARREST THE FOLLOWING PERSONS,**" read the headline. "The most important persons of the past Marxist regime are implicated in the Red Conspiracy and economic scandals. It is imperative to interrogate them in order to arrive at the real truth, such as their projected mass assassinations of the Armed Forces and anti-Marxist opposition, and the robbery of the national treasury."

Among the military's 13 most wanted criminals was Mickey, the ex-leader of New Havana. When we had first seen him there we had no idea that the quiet fellow hanging around on the edge of the crowd with eyes downcast, occasionally kicking up dust with the toe of one shoe, was the camp leader. When he was finally introduced he warned, "No pictures!" One day, when he had decided he could trust us, he simply turned up in the finder of Ted's camera.

Mickey, an electrician, was one of the few national MIR leaders without a university education. He remained the elected head of New Havana during the entire three years of its existence, although other MIR officers were ousted in surprise votes. The opposition press portrayed "El Mickey" as a wild man, and reported exploits like his dumping of garbage at the local town hall to force its collection from the camp.

After the coup Mickey survived underground for one and one-half years, despite the wide display of his photograph and a substantial reward offered for his capture. Mickey's life ended when the DINA (secret police) broke into a safe house in the port city of Valparaíso, put a bullet in his head and dumped his body on a street.

left: El Mercurio's front page calls for the capture of 13 people most wanted by the ruling junta, including Allende's secretary, cabinet ministers, heads of formerly legal parties and MIR leaders, including Mickey (in circle).

right: Mickey, Carmen Jarpa and daughter in front of their house in New Havana.

MICKEY, 1972: Housing in Chile isn't a right, it's a privilege, a luxury. And a squatter—who has no house, who's backward and crippled when it comes to job skills—is absolutely explosive. The most violent clashes of recent years have involved squatters who were willing to hurl themselves into the streets where some of them died.

Until the end of the 1960s the Christian Democrats were clobbering them, but with elections coming up, they let up. The traditional parties of the left were only interested in their own electoral needs, so the MIR [Revolutionary Left Movement, organized by students to the left of Communists and Socialists] moved out of the universities. Shantytown people were our first mass base and seizing land was the most revolutionary thing we could do.

Our first toma [land takeover] in 1969 was very revolutionary. We ate together, slept together, stood guard together. We were hungry, miserable and cold together. There was a common food pot, and anybody who wanted to could guard the camp, even women. As news of our experience spread it inspired other tomas.

To get our land, inside of a couple of months we conducted sit-ins at Catholic University, the University of Chile, the Ministries of Housing and Engineering and some fancy new apartment towers. Plenty of luxury housing was going up.

Just before Allende was elected a group of women went on a six-day hunger strike in the doorway of Congress. Some squatters battled their way through the lines of cops, so the riot police responded by clubbing them. All this produced a state of alert in Santiago because the public saw us as a revolutionary army and the rightist press made a big scandal out of it.

The right wanted to screw up the election. In order to avoid playing into their hands, the MIR moderated its actions. Anyway, by that time we'd mostly gotten the land we wanted.

Allende won by a small margin. The opposition still controlled Congress and the country was in limbo, so we turned to our immediate problems—getting electricity, water, utilities and roads so the settlers could occupy the space they'd been promised. The new government pledged to build 100,000 houses in 14 months, worker participation in the economy, a half-liter of milk for every child every day, and elimination of the riot police.

Seventeen-hundred families from three previous tomas moved here, and there was an overnight change from attacking the government. When they kept their word on the riot police,

our military discipline dropped and the popular militia just disappeared. Perhaps it was just as well, because it had been born deformed, with insignia, slogan-yelling and an ostentatious display of clubs. That may have been fine for fighting cops, but then they turned against the settlers themselves whenever there were squabbles or petty differences.

In general, squatters have nothing to say about what kind of housing they get. The government plans them, the government gives them. The Chamber of Construction—that's the Mafia of the construction industry—still controls supplies and builds 80 percent of the housing. When it came to our permanent houses we weren't going to let private enterprise come in and screw us, so we turned ourselves into a state housing enterprise. The settlers work on construction, the government provides supplies and pays the salaries.

We didn't foresee some of the problems. Before now, only the MIR could meet peoples' needs; now the government steps in with all kinds of services. Before now, the MIR could expel anybody from the camp; now, without a hostile government to confront, our authority is eroding and we can't do that any more.

Overnight, our relations with the government changed. During Frei's administration, when shantytown people asked for an interview with his housing minister it was like going to church for a handout. Now the new bureaucrats in the ministry welcome you. "Hello there, compañero. Please sit down. How's it going? Have a cigarette. Let's talk." Then they fuck you over just the same.

right: Santiago, 1972. Mickey (center right) shouting at a demonstration. He became notorious in Santiago when the opposition press featured his militant exploits, designed to embarrass authorities into providing services for the camp.

Carmen Jarpa lives with her second husband, two sons, a daughter and two grandchildren, in one of the cement block houses erected for New Havana's residents, most of which were turned over to strangers by the new military rulers.

One of the neighborhood's four public telephones sits on a high stool near the open window of Carmen's living room, where anyone who needs to make a call must reach in from the street. Whenever that poses an inconvenience, as it did when we sat talking at the lace-covered table near the window, Carmen closes the window and hangs up an "Out of Order" sign.

To supplement her husband's income from a small store, Carmen knits. From her clacking needles come snowy angoras with delicate beading, suitable for cocktail parties in neighborhoods very unlike her own, and thick sweaters sporting primitive landscapes for skiing on elegant Andean slopes. She earns very little for her considerable skill.

Her son Julio, 21, separated from his wife, and living there with his two children, is irritated by people who come to visit Carmen. He says, "I remember how my mother suffered, how she took in washing to make a living. This family has nothing more to do with politics. It devotes itself only to survival."

CARMEN, 1989: September 11th [1973] was a frightening day. On radio and television they began calling for people to turn in Mickey, saying he was one of the most wanted criminals in Chile. He went into hiding on the very first day. The last time I ever saw him was two days later, when they lifted the curfew and he came home, but we had no time to talk about anything. He only said he was going to stay away so nothing would happen to me, and told me to get rid of all his clothing. Still, I was certain he'd come back one day.

When it was almost time for me to have the baby [Alejandro Jr. was born September 21st] some friends tried to bring me to my mother, but her neighborhood was surrounded by soldiers. We went to one of Mickey's uncles instead, where it seemed safer.

Five days after Alejandro was born I was back. They came for me in the middle of the night and pushed me around with their machine guns, asking where my husband was. I said I didn't know, so they asked my daughters, who went like this [she shrugs] with their little shoulders. They broke the windows and smashed the baby's crib. Then they shot through the door and almost hit a neighbor who was passing by.

They wanted to know how I met Mickey, exactly what he

did in the campamento, the names of every person he knew. I told them the leaders were all from outside the camp and nobody knew their true names, only nicknames. Finally they let go of me when I said I had to breastfeed my son.

In February 1975 I was watching television when they started rolling the names of fugitives and exiles on the screen. The very last one was Mickey. They said he was dead, so I went to a lawyer to file a petition to find out if he was dead or alive. It took almost a year before they let me have his death certificate, and it said, "Place of death: On a public way, by bullet wound." Like they'd found him in the street. Later, a compañero told me he'd been there in the safe house in Valparaíso when the DINA [secret police] broke in and shot Mickey in the mouth. They never let me see his body.

I was already a widow when I met the man who's now my husband, and started living with him. I couldn't feed my kids alone and I married him in 1976. Because he wasn't involved in politics, people started saying right off that I was disgracing Mickey, that I was a traitor for looking for another compañero.

During all the time I was alone, not a single one of them came to see me, not even to leave a piece of bread. Now that things are changing they justify their not coming around by saying they were afraid. But I'm not interested in them. They are hypocrites who turned their backs on me.

right: Carmen at home in New Dawn.

above: Two women carry prefabricated panels supplied by Allende's housing ministry to help New Havana improve its ramshackle shelters.

top right: Construction of this communal dining hall is considered a step in the liberation of women. Other public structures going up at the same time include a nursery school, mothers' center and clinic.

bottom right: One of every three workers in the community housing enterprise which is building the permanent houses comes from the camp's formerly unskilled unemployed, now training to become construction workers.

far right: In a shantytown which is not so well-organized, white collar professionals, government bureaucrats and students are spending the day hauling rocks, digging holes and helping to improve the houses of some waiting families.

above: Volunteers and trainees, supervised by National Health Service professionals, staff the clinic and help with local programs for pre-natal care, sanitation and public health education.

right: A Health Front puppet show. The villains—Infection, Mud, Garbage and Flies—plot against the people. Children destroy the Flies by cleaning up Garbage and Mud, thus foiling Infection.

top: The Education Ministry provides teachers to staff the extinct buses which they have refurbished to serve as temporary classrooms.

bottom: Many tiny businesses exist in the shacks. In this house two entrepreneurs turn shirt collars and give haircuts.

right: At the dedication of the New Havana Mother's Center small girls in tutus dance for Hortensia Bussi de Allende (called Tencha by all), the president's wife, who has come to present an ambulance to the clinic. The Master of Ceremonies is Aníbal.

CENTRO DE MADRES
NUEVA HABANA
MUJERES
REVOLUCIONARIAS
revolucion
HASTA LA VICTORIA SIEMPRE

Cecilia Bernal and Aníbal were shantytown dwellers who were so articulate that many foreigners assumed them to be university graduates who had moved into the camp by political choice. He laughed and pointed out that his mother, sister, kid brother and other relatives all lived there too. Cecilia was a dedicated rank-and-file activist.

CECILIA, 1972: Are men and women equal here? Look, in the top leadership there's only one woman. Some of them say they don't like politics or they don't understand it. It's embedded in a woman that she must be a slave to her husband and kids. We say, "Look, to make this community work we all have to join in, even if it's only for a few hours."

For example, volunteers tend sick children in a warm room where they can be better cared for than in our unheated houses. At a block meeting I say, "Compañera, we need you for a shift." She doesn't answer, the husband answers for her, "She can't! She has four kids." We have women with nine kids who do it, only they keep it a secret from their husbands.

When it doesn't affect them directly, men don't help. If somebody said that construction would stop because there's no more money, they'd pound the table and yell, "Mobilize the women, the old people, the children." Why are we women so timid, so conservative? We're ignorant. We believe everything we're told.

When men were in charge of the ambulance, they messed up. Now that the drivers are women, things are better. Why shouldn't we work on home building too? We're planning a workshop so that women who must work don't only do laundry for foreigners. They can knit, embroider. Maybe we could sell the work to gringos who come to look us over.

The married state doesn't count for much here. There must be a thousand couples not married under bourgeois law. My compañero and I got together eight years ago, and we have three children. Once I was once married legitimately, in a church, but then the marriage failed, and I later became a widow.

What's important is a good relationship, understanding each other. Still, people are scandalized. If we lived elsewhere I couldn't say we aren't married. "Aieeeee, immoral!" Here, that attitude has passed into history. Aníbal and I are like all couples. We argue, we fight, sometimes we even hit each other. Friendship means fights.

What we cannot allow is drinking. A guy gets drunk, fights, *insults his neighbors, beats his wife and kids. The Vigilance Front puts him in a room till the monkey is gone. In the morning they tell him, "Next time you'll be expelled." If he doesn't straighten up he'll have to leave, with his family, because if we let them stay, he comes sneaking back. And he doesn't want to lose his chance at the little house we're building.*

Bourgeois women—sociologists, psychologists—come here to study us. They ask questions, they never contradict anything we say. When they finish investigating and get paid, they don't come around any more. We might see one later, giving someone a tour. One gringo came here to make a movie, even interviewed people in my house. Later I heard that his movie was shown in Santiago and in other countries, but he never showed it around here.

Before I came here I had a good house, but it wasn't mine, it was the priest's. I was the church caretaker, so they gave me a kitchen with gas, a bathroom with hot water, and a salary besides. I gave it up for the possibility that in this place we can become indivisible and create something marvelous.

right: 1971. Cecilia and daughter Ivalú, Aníbal and son Andy. In the evenings Aníbal and a committee tabulate the camp census at the table by lamplight. He laughs about the pictures on the wall. "This one's mine (Ché) and that one's hers (The Last Supper)."

CECILIA, Santiago, 1989: *Oh, that was a beautiful time. Every-thing seemed possible. Until a week after the coup our organ-ization remained intact. We were still hoping to occupy the houses on November 4th. People kept working on their projects as if everything would turn out well. But it didn't.*

Soldiers arrived in tanks and trucks and started to take the leaders away to the stadium—one by one. We were surrounded. Everywhere, mílicos, mílicos, mílicos. A few people turned into "sapos"—toads, informers—perhaps not on their own blood relatives, but we had been like a family. They identified people. "He was a block leader, he was a campamento leader."

So much pressure. Soldiers with pictures, "You know this one?" Somebody would answer, "Yes, but he's gone away to Argentina," although he was still there. That's exactly what happened with Aníbal: he was warned to flee because the mílicos were after him with a photo. It was a difficult time. I didn't know where he was. Everything was chaos, anarchy.

I left my house too, but stayed within the camp. First, I gave away everything—beds, tables, dishes—and took the kids to a friend's house. After soldiers came twice in one night my friend said, "I can't keep you anymore. You're a danger to us." I destroyed everything that might be incriminating—documents, photos, everything—and went to the priest's house for a while. Finally, my presence endangered him also.

Before he went away Aníbal and I talked to a judge who told us, "You two must get married because under the law, a wife can't be arrested just for being a wife, while a live-in companion can." The wedding was two witnesses, no ring, and Aníbal got away to Argentina. The judge said to us, "Well, this is my last wedding. The military is throwing me out." A couple of years ago I saw him downtown, selling combs in the street.

The church helped me get new ID cards for the kids and myself, but when I went for my passport somebody said, "You're Cecilia Bernal? There's a warrant for you." I said, "Who, me? I don't understand what you're talking about," and left fast.

A church lawyer said, "We'll go together for your passport. You will say that for twelve years you have lived in the same house as your mother, that they have made a mistake, that other people have the same name." He told them I had never lived in New Havana, and this time they gave me the passport. Two days later the kids and I were in the airport.

There I was, talking to myself, "I must stay here. I can't pull out like a rat." I answered myself, "What will the children do without a mother? I can't abandon them." Maternal instincts are stronger than any cause. So I went.

We stayed in Argentina two years. Aníbal was a social worker in the church of Santo Domingo, he was a construction worker, he washed cars. I was ticketseller and wardrobe mistress in a theatre. The kids had missed a year of school in Chile. In Argentina they led a normal life, but we told them, "Out there it's Argentina. In here it's Chile. Chilean food, Chilean music, Chilean talk."

We worked and worked, made lots of friends, lived in a beautiful house with a big patio. Oh, I felt like a queen. But the situation was very unstable. A coup was coming to Argentina too. Many Chileans were arrested [at the request of the Chilean government]. I had a big house so Chileans started coming, even people from New Havana. Beds here, beds there. Pretty soon there were 25 people living there and the neighbors started getting curious. "Your house looks like the Chilean embassy," they'd say.

The military came around. "Why so many people?" "Look," we'd answer, "they're refugees with no place to go." In the end we also had to flee—to a convent. It was fenced-in and we had food, but we weren't safe, so we went to the United Nations, which gave us three choices. A Latin American country: we picked Mexico. A socialist country: we picked Romania. Any country: we picked Canada, never imagining that's where we would end up.

In February 1976, Argentine summer, we left. First stop: Santiago. But they didn't let us leave the plane. It was painful to sit there that night. There were two more stops before we landed in Vancouver. The immigration lady asked my compañero why we had come, and began filling out the form. "How much money do you have?" "Five dollars American." "What do you have to declare?" "What shall I declare to you? My compañera? Four children? Twelve years of marriage in four suitcases?" "Welcome to Canada," she said. "Right this way!"

right: Santiago, 1991. Cecilia lives in a small house with a garden and a high fence in a working class district. Weekends and holidays she drives her tiny van to a good spot to sell food or ice cream. Here she serves hot dogs and coffee at a political rally with her mother (at right).

We didn't feel the cold in our bodies because the airport was warm, but our souls were cold. We didn't know the language, we didn't know anybody, we didn't know what to do. They told us to fly to Calgary. In Calgary they told us to wait for another flight. The children were pleading, "No more airplanes."

When we finally landed in Medicine Hat there was no jetway, so we walked through the snow dressed for summer. The kids were jumping up and down yelling, "Snow! Snow." A big man with a pipe showed up, asking, "Who is Mr. Moonoze [Muñoz]?" Varinia, my youngest daughter, wanted to know, "Who is he? My grandfather?"

The next morning was the worst. I don't even like thinking about it. I got up very early and looked out of the motel window. There were no houses, nothing. I ran to the bathroom, and from the little window I saw flat, flat land, snow everywhere and a highway. Far, far away, a big smokestack. "Aníbal!" I woke him up, "There are no people, there's not a soul, and we have to live here?" He said, "Calm down." Then Mr. Pearson came to take us to an enormous Woolworth's to buy warm clothes.

The following Wednesday Aníbal went to work in the brick factory. That was the smokestack I had seen. They gave him a heavy jacket, gloves, safety boots and helmet. Carts full of bricks came along and he lifted them off, put them down, lifted them off, put them down. Hard work. I washed dishes in a restaurant, made pizzas, planted flowers in a greenhouse.

Soon a Chilean came to visit, the only one in Medicine Hat. Somebody to communicate with. Eleven of us would go out walking. People would stop their cars. "Where are you from?" "No speak English" was all we could answer. People were very interested in our lives. They didn't even know where Chile was.

When we moved to Calgary we had a nice house. Rented, not bought. Why would we buy a house? We never intended to stay. Chileans who live abroad always have two suitcases ready. I would go to the Salvation Army and see some sheets. "Oh, how pretty. I want them. For Chile." And I put them in the suitcase. When we arrived in Canada we said it would be for three years. Then five. But I never thought of staying. Never!

I came back here with Varinia in 1982 to visit my family, having decided that if I had changed, I would go back to Canada forever. If I had not changed I would stay in Chile for good. A change would have been if I'd thought, "It's so ugly, so many flies, so much dust, so much dirt." But it seemed so normal. Normal, as if I'd never been away. I told Varinia we would stay in Chile for six months, and if she didn't like it we'd return to Canada. But I was lying.

Of course there are changes, reactions to all the years of terrible oppression. People are cold, suspicious. "Why did you leave? Why did you come back?" But when the airplane door opens and you get out, there's your air, your sun, your willow trees. You walk down the road, your people are working the land. Yours, yours, yours. I'll never leave Chile again.

Varinia was 15 when they returned to Chile. Within a year she had become an unwed mother, but with Cecilia's help she continued to do well at a public high school, although she complained that she was repeating things they taught in seventh grade in Vancouver. She said that a decent education in Chile was available only to those who can pay for it. Varinia was always certain she would be a sociologist, but after high school it proved impossible to raise enough money for tuition at the University of Chile. In 1992, undoubtedly helped by her good looks and good English, she was hired at a fancy new tourist hotel owned by a U.S. chain.

Aníbal, after a couple of attempts to resettle in Chile, returned to Canada, where the other children live and work.

VARINIA: My mom had warned me we'd be poor again, and things would seem very different. My cousins said we were crazy for leaving Canada, and at first I really hated it here. Now I feel very Chilean. Chileans abroad who think they're so well off, what are they? They're still rotos [ragged ones], only now they're rotos with money.

From the time we came back, I've had three best friends. One knew nothing, one is the daughter of a disappeared, one is the daughter of a colonel. When she asked her father what the military had done, he said it was all lies. Now she understands and doesn't ask him.

right: 1989. Varinia and her daughter Tatiana.

Viviana Quiroz, an enthusiastic member of the Vigilance Front in the old days, went into exile with six of her children, all of whom are now Swedish citizens. Her draft-age son Nelson had to stay behind. In 1989 she came back to visit him.

VIVIANA, 1989: Yes, it's my neighborhood, my camp, only dirtier, with more miserable-looking kids. Maybe there's some of the same feeling of solidarity, I can't tell. What I do know is that I'll never come back here. I was a person who lived in misery day and night, who changed her whole existence. I'm doing very well now. I have a car, a telephone and a two-story house. That's a change from the earth to heaven.

left: New Havana, 1972. Liquor, blamed for wife and child abuse and bad health, is forbidden. This drunk was knocked out when he started an argument, and carried off to sober up. When he wakes up the Vigilance Committee will give him a lecture. Then, if he does not reform, he and his family will be tossed out.

above: Viviana, 1972, holding the leather truncheon of the Vigilance Committee.

right: 1989. Old friend Oscar Cáceres comes running to greet Viviana when he hears she is back. Nelson (at right) was drafted, deserted after being disciplined for shooting in the air instead of directly at demonstrators, and thrown out of the army. Today he collects scrap newspaper and peddles it to butchers for wrapping. His ten year-old son lives with Viviana in Sweden.

above: New Dawn, 1989. Oscar, one of the oldest New Havana activists, ran against MIR candidates in a camp election in the old days—and won. He says his house is too shabby for entertaining and invites us instead to the house of a neighbor who grew up in the camp. The house still has its original dirt floor.

right: 1989. One of a small number of children enrolled in pre-school programs of a social service agency dedicated to educating slum children and training their mothers as day care workers. The girl holds an "arpillera." In the workshops of the Vicariate of Solidarity of the church these appliques became the chief means of support for mothers and wives of prisoners and the disappeared, and an art form to tell their stories.

On a rainy midnight in 1970, seven hundred adults and children swarmed over the estate of a local businessman in Talcahuano, an industrial suburb of Concepción, Chile's third largest city. By dawn the ground was covered with makeshift shelters. A tight ring of police kept out people who had sneaked off to go to work, and friends and relatives delivering food.

The owner stripped his private chapel and 42-room house of everything except a wall safe, reinforced the gates with chicken wire and fled, leaving behind only a sullen black dog and the nervous housekeeper Clementina to guard his property.

Javier Navarro, the leader of the encampment, who had been a priest until he decided that "Marxism is the highest stage of Catholicism," made his rounds of Campamento Lenin like an old-fashioned, benevolent politician, followed by children and dogs, listening to problems, settling disputes. In contrast to the elaborate web of fronts and volunteers in New Havana, life at Lenin was chaotic. Individual privies sprouted on every plot, and anyone who needed lumber or fuel could cut down a tree.

Navarro knew that the outgoing Frei government wanted to avoid election-eve battles, so he traveled to Santiago to bargain with officials. A deal was struck. The government called off the police siege and negotiated with the owner for transfer of the land; Navarro agreed to take the blame, and was sentenced to 147 days in jail for trespassing, which he never served.

When we first encountered Navarro he boasted of his camp's feistiness and invited us to visit him. We arrived in Concepción, settled in a shabby hotel and took a bus to the camp, but nobody in the jovial crowd that surrounded us seemed to know where Navarro was. They invited us to look around anyway, following along and asking, "Are you with the Peace Corps?" "The CIA?"

On the bus back to town we were trailed conspicuously by a small boy who tried to make himself invisible on the back bench. He debarked bravely at out hotel, but began crying as soon as his feet touched the street. It was almost dark, he didn't know where he was, they had given him only enough money for one way. We paid his return fare, and when he got back to the camp he helped establish our credibility by reporting that our hotel was not too bourgeois.

right: 1972. Ex-priest Javier Navarro is followed by children as he makes his rounds. Some people resent his style, which reminds them of an old-style "caudillo" (chief).

Navarro appeared the next morning to assign Hilda, a widow with eight children from first grade to draft-age, to look after us. Hilda would get up at one each morning, drive her horse and wagon to the produce market to buy vegetables, peddle them on the street, and be back by noon to sell her surplus and attend meetings. Two walls of Hilda's main room were decorated, one by pictures of Asian revolutionaries, the other by cutouts from fashion magazines.

Hilda kept coaxing us to eat and her friend Lucy reinforced her: "Skinny is ugly. Fat is beautiful." Both women vied for Navarro's attention, affectionately calling him Gordo—Fatso. They chastized us for turning down cigarettes because "everybody knows that only momios (reactionaries) don't smoke."

A few weeks later Ted returned to observe a national convention of militant homeless people. He slept in the bed of Bernardo Cárdenas, who worked nights at the gas plant and slept days. His wife Ida had originally come from the far south for medical care, and they had remained in Concepción. Bernardo could never say no to Navarro's requests for the common good, so his living room was piled with cement sacks and leaflets which threatened to push the family out. Ida smiled, and continued to cook empanadas and cazuela, the ubiquitous Chilean turnovers and chicken soup. She asked, "What good will the revolution be if my kids don't survive?"

Their house had been the original post office. The plastic sheets and torn blankets which shielded glassless windows were no match for wind and rain. Political posters covered cracks in the walls. Ted wrote in a letter, "Ida remade Bernardo's bed for me in the main room and left a candle and matches. The puppy kept licking my hand or foot, or whatever was hanging out of the bed. Ida left hot embers in the brazier, but the room was cold and the wall next to my bed was damp. The next morning I had a dozen bites I thought were mosquito bites. After four days I was covered with them, and everybody laughed because they are all immune to fleas."

left: 1972. Ida and Bernardo Cárdenas at home. The three children are Joanna, Vladimir and Axel.

right: 1972. Dinner time in the Cárdenas family's main room, next to the camp's cement and leaflets which Bernardo agreed to keep.

After 17 years we returned. At Bernardo's old union a secretary who had been hired by the military, dazzling in polka dots, matching beads, earrings, belt, shoes and thick lipstick, denied knowing anyone of Bernardo's ilk.

We canvassed the old district, and were invited into a tiny house which quickly filled with neighbors who told us about the people in our photographs. Lucy had moved far away and died "of natural causes" before she reached forty. Hilda had suffered a stroke and died just before we arrived. Navarro had moved to England after a night-time escape over the wall of the British Embassy.

As for Bernardo, some people thought they recognized him. Two women led us to a walled yard full of rusting metal. Ida answered our knock, then thunderstruck and still silent, led us inside where Vladimir, now 21, was cleaning an ancient Fiat engine with gasoline. Nadiezhda, Axel, Joanna and her husband appeared with three small children. By the time Bernardo, covered with mechanic's grease, opened the door, the scene resembled a party.

There had not been enough jail cells when he was arrested, so with 400 others he was confined to a drained swimming pool that was so crowded that they stood all day and were let out only at night to sleep on the ground. Ida sold all their possessions for food.

Upon his release the following year Bernardo, a skilled machinist, found himself unemployable because his release papers branded him a common criminal, not only a political one, for seizing land. To survive, he became an itinerant mechanic, specializing in patching up the worn-out cars of the poor.

Vladimir, whose name alone disqualified him for a job, worked with him, mostly outdoors but also inside the house. An open pan of powerful solvent sat on the floor near the kitchen. The yard was a repository for parts and scrap. The house—not the original shack but hardly better—still lacked an indoor toilet.

The family took us on a tour of the old camp streets, where nothing seemed familiar. The trees were gone, the pond where we had once seen a man shoot a duck for dinner was a stagnant, fetid puddle. Some hovels had grown a second story, most were protected by strong fences, and a small number were concrete block houses built by the original community as permanent housing.

In the evening we crowded around the kitchen table eating bread and meat, talking of failures, the future, and the death of communism. It was late when we rose to leave but Ida was upset, "How can you go? I haven't made the empanadas yet."

right: 1989. Bernardo is flanked by Jesus and campaign posters for Aylwin and local candidates. The church helped Ida keep the family together when Bernardo was in prison and blacklisted.

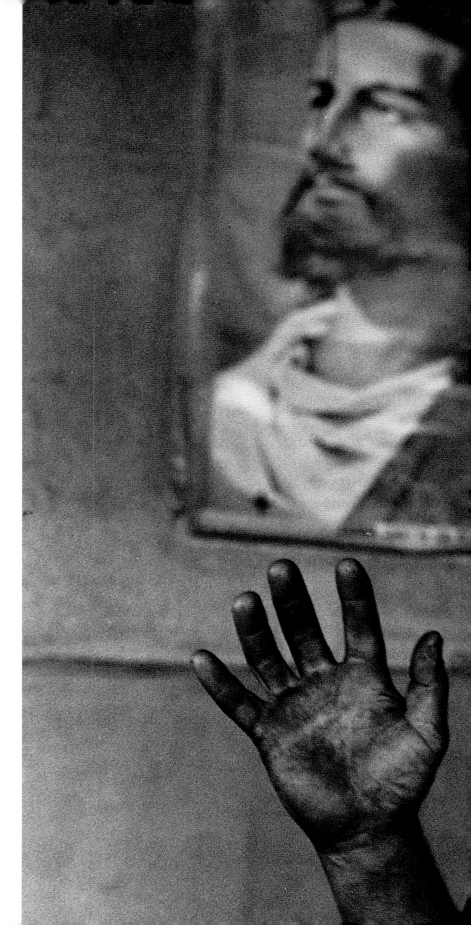

In 1972 Tuly Ulloa and Ramón Riquelme, educated and from well-off families, were living and working with homeless people in a shantytown. Ramón is a poet. When we first met him he stated, "The times are too urgent for poems, the dangers too great."

When Tuly's father vanished in 1930 her mother kept it a secret from her that he had been caught and thrown into the sea while trying to escape to Argentina during the dictatorship of President Ibáñez.

The small encampment of the homeless and unemployed where Tuly and Ramón lived in 1972 impinged on a wealthy section of Concepción. "This really bothers the 'beautiful people' in the neighborhood, and they hate Ramón, but they hate me even more because my father was a landowner. They think Ramón influences me, when really it's the other way round."

When we returned to Chile at the end of 1989 we had little hope of finding them again until an acquaintance, leafing through the photographs we carried everywhere, recognized Ramón. "I've seen that man! His wife is a potter. They live in Quinchamalí."

Home telephones are still rare, so despite our lack of faith in her identification of a 17 year-old picture, we set out immediately on the Pan American highway, turning west some 400 miles later onto a washboard road that wound into the mountains, where we found a weathered plank marking the turnoff.

Neighbors directed us to a rustic house surrounded by roses and cherry trees, from which Ramón and Tuly emerged onto a deep porch, embraced us and led us past greenhouse pottery racks into an unheated primitive kitchen. A charcoal brazier glowed on the rough floor beneath the kitchen table. Within minutes our feet were warm, we were drinking strong tea and hearing how Ted's photograph of Ramón had been seized in a raid on their empty house, then used by the secret police to hunt for him. Neither of them acted as if our visit was odd or surprising.

Ramón spent three years in prison. Upon his release, Tuly began to work with the Catholic Church. In 1983 she was one of 20 women brave enough to protest disappearances on the streets of Chillan, the nearest city. As demonstrations continued, the number of women grew to over a hundred, and Quinchamalí voted two to one against Pinochet in the plebiscite.

left: Ramón Riquelme in 1972.

right: 1991. Tuly Ulloa and Ramón Riquelme in their garden.

TULY, 1989: Our community was in a strategic spot, so perhaps after the coup the military thought we would be trying to get explosives from the quarry near us, where they stored them. They surrounded our camp; a helicopter kept flying overhead— ten minutes to the quarry, ten minutes back, ten minutes to the quarry, ten minutes back. We were all terrified, and nobody knew what to do.

RAMON: The military expected armed resistance from us. In reality, everybody was asking, "Where are the weapons?" Everyone was so certain that the leaders must have prepared some grand strategy that they sent a compañero to find out what we were supposed to do. He never returned.

Since we had no guidance, it was decided that those who ran the greatest risk must leave. The next day Tuly and I went to her mother's house in Quinchamalí. It was like switching a railroad car from one train to another—different customs, a different way of life. I didn't know anybody, and I never ventured outdoors because arrest awaited me there. The work we had done was perfectly legal. Suddenly it had become a crime.

After a couple of weeks a lieutenant and six soldiers came for me in a pickup truck. I didn't resist. They drove me to regimental headquarters in Chillán where, as I was getting out of the truck, somebody called out, "Hey you! You're the one who burned the theatre in Concepción."

They blindfolded me and marched me over a river with 15 or 20 other prisoners—I thought it was a river because I could hear water flowing—and led us into a ditch to wait. It must have been a ditch, because they threw rocks and urinated on us from above. The first time they took me to be interrogated I knew we were inside a building because when I couldn't walk fast enough, I was slammed against a solid wall. Somebody was barking like a dog, or perhaps it was a recording. They kept threatening my genitals and when I flinched, they kicked me.

The blindfold slipped a bit before they undressed me to apply the electric current, and I saw a tall fellow wearing a hood and boots. "What political party do you belong to?" I said I didn't have a party. He said I was lying and hit me. They kept shocking me, and asking why and how I had burned the theatre. When I realized there was no escape I admitted, "Yes! I burned the theatre by leaping over the wall and setting the fire with paraffin."

They knew it was a lie. I was already in Quinchamalí at the time, and anyone can see that I have difficulty just walking. I

feared their justice system left only two possibilities; they would imprison me, or they would kill me and leave my body in the river or street. I didn't sleep for the first week.

TULY: I didn't know what had happened to Ramón. My family was so frightened they prevented me even from looking. I contacted somebody I knew in the military who told me to send my mother, since there was a warrant for my arrest. She found Ramón. A cousin who lived nearby brought him food and clothing. After four months I said I was going to visit even if they arrested me. They didn't bother.

He finally got out after 16 months because I enlisted the help of a conservative newspaper editor who had a good reputation with the authorities. He wrote a long article which said, "Ramón Riquelme was my student. He is a poet who loves art and culture, and could never have burned the theatre."

RAMON: The military prosecutor protested that it was a mistake to release a man who could think and write. He said people like me are the most dangerous kind. I recovered, but for those with me who were tortured and died, there has to be justice. The guilty must be prosecuted, fairly, without the humiliations we suffered. My spirit can't seek vengeance.

In the hospital, three years after my release, a nurse I had never seen before said, "I'm certain that I know you." It turned out that when he was a young boy doing his compulsory military service, I was marching blindfolded. On the way to a torture session, when my shoe fell off on the footbridge, he had stopped me to put it back on. I still recall the sensation of someone tenderly placing the shoe on my foot.

TULY: Ramón was arrested again as we were getting on a train. I had gone up the steps ahead of him and didn't even notice that the DINA [secret police] had grabbed him until the train was underway. By pure luck, he was saved by a soldier I had met previously when he came to transport me to the city for questioning. During the ride he said, "I only drive the truck," so we got to talking. When he saw Ramón at headquarters he began shouting, "What the hell are you doing here?" and ordered him to get out. If he hadn't been there that day, Ramón might have disappeared forever.

right: A small traditional black pottery horseman sits in Tuly and Ramón's kitchen window. When Tuly returned to Quinchamalí, called "the town where the earth speaks," she helped organize a gallery and marketing cooperative for the potters.

The Disputed Land

Chilean agriculture languished in the 1920's, when the rural gentry invested in factories and moved to the cities, keeping their farms as retreats, but planting few crops. Production stagnated, and Chile soon had to import food.

Three-quarters of the farmland was in "latifundios"—estates of over 2,500 acres—where early efforts to organize farmworkers were easily defeated, and the owners controlled every aspect of a peasant's life. On much of the remaining land generations of subdivision among sons had created "minifundos"—farms too tiny and poor to be productive.

In 1964 Christian Democratic candidate Eduardo Frei won the presidency on a platform that included land reform. Frei promised to relocate one third of Chile's 300,000 landless families, but by the end of his six-year term only 25,000 of them had been moved onto land reform settlements. Many of the farmworkers then switched their allegiance to Allende, who had promised more extensive changes.

Using laws already on the books, Allende's new government proceeded to expropriate more land in six months than had been taken in the previous six years. The giant latifundios were dismantled, although their old owners still controlled a strong press and radio network, with allies in parliament and an unchanged judiciary. The stage was set for conflict.

After they took power in 1973, the military promptly handed the land back into private hands, and provided the owners with agricultural loans that were almost gifts. Exports of lumber and fruit, much of it from trees planted in the days of land reform, brought prosperity to the big landholders in the 1980s.

Today's farmworkers are once again without land, but the old feudal mentality is gone. After the experience of running their own farms they no longer tip their hats or tremble when the boss passes by. The grip of the past has not been totally restored.

Hearken to me a while, and having heard me
Decide whether or not our rebellion is justified.

When you first appeared in our country
Demanding obedience to the King of Spain
Many of us were willing to submit
                 in exchange for being left in peace.
It was not long before your greed
                 trampled everything underfoot.
You made us work but did not feed us.
You left us to die in the mines
                 without the consolation of our own people.
You plundered our settlements
                 and took unto yourselves our women and children.

If a single Indian remains alive he will perish
                 with a weapon in his hand
Rather than live under your subjugation.

From the words of Quiavelo,
an Araucano elder, 1629

Chile, the last country to be invaded by the Spanish Crown, was the only one whose indigenous population, the Araucanos, offered fierce and unrelenting resistance for centuries. Pedro de Valdivia and an armor-clad band of adventurers rode into Chile from the north in 1541. In battle after battle, thousands of Araucanos armed with spears and pikes, fought mounted invaders armed with guns, and were slaughtered.

Then Lautaro, a teenager, who had been Valdivia's page and knew his weaknesses, returned to his own tribe. His strategy was to exhaust the seemingly invincible enemy, and for a time it worked, although at high cost. For their first battle Lautaro chose a Spanish supply road along the Andes. Waves of Araucanos attacked, suffering heavy casualties, and survivors fled to the steep crags where heavily-armored men on horseback could not follow. Fresh groups then took their places.

right: Cautín Province, 1971. Señora Francisca Curipán, who owned a tiny farm, was too frightened to protest when the landowner next door moved the boundary fence at night, bit by bit. After Allende was elected she moved it back with the help of neighbors. The sign says, "Mapuche, Recover Your Usurped Land."

In this manner, the Spanish army was destroyed. Legend has it that molten gold was poured into Valdivia's mouth and his thigh bones were turned into battle flutes.

Although Lautaro was killed at the age of 21 by the arrow of an Indian mercenary, the Indians continued their guerrilla warfare. Undefeated in war, they nevertheless lost their population to disease, overwork and famine. Enslaved in the gold mines and later driven onto reserves, they became the despised people of Chile, stereotyped as filthy, lazy and immoral. Their descendants are called Mapuches—people of the land.

When the decimated indigenous population began to increase again in the 20th century, there was no room on the reservations for expansion. Mapuche farms, subdivided again and again within families, had become too small and primitive to be fruitful. With few draught animals and insufficient water, Mapuche farmers practiced a haphazard form of agriculture. Their fallow fields were overgrazed by sheep, leached by rain, blown away by wind. On planted fields, seed was poor and crops not always suitable for the soil. Fertilizer, when the peasant could afford it, was often improperly applied. They mortgaged their harvests and had to consume their surplus to survive.

The Mapuches of Cautín province, scene of the Araucano revolts, became the poorest and most impatient of all Chilean peasants. During the Allende years they grabbed farms without waiting for official procedures, prompting some landlords to make their farms unworkable, even slaughtering their own cattle or marching them over the Andes to Argentina. Others reclaimed their territory with armed gangs.

Even pleas from President Allende and strong disapproval from many leftist supporters did not slow down the land seizures. The Mapuches joined any effort which held out a promise, however faint, of restoring their ancestral lands.

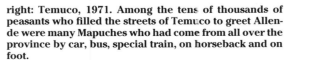

right: Temuco, 1971. Among the tens of thousands of peasants who filled the streets of Temuco to greet Allende were many Mapuches who had come from all over the province by car, bus, special train, on horseback and on foot.

When Ted sought permission to photograph Mapuches on several of the "tomas" (tomar—to take or seize) in Cautín Province, he was greeted at every locked gate by hostile, club-wielding guards. That night, as we were talking over the problem at a bus stop in Temuco, the provincial capital, an offer of help came from the darkness, and we were led through unlit streets to a seedy student hangout where a fellow who introduced himself as Titín volunteered to guide Ted to a farm.

The next morning, en route by bus to the farm called Rucalán, Titín told of being a runaway at the age of nine, and spending several years begging and stealing before going to work in a textile mill. A strike sent him to jail, and his cellmate introduced him to Marx and Trotsky. To demonstrate his revolutionary commitment he snapped open his briefcase for a glimpse of an ancient revolver inside.

It turned out that the farm was on the opposite shore of the broad Imperial River from the bus stop. Titín shouted and jumped and waved in the direction of a tiny white patch until something began to move on the water—a small skinny boy in a leaky boat who was coming across to get them. As the boy rowed them back, the shadows which appeared on the white patch slowly resolved themselves into the face of Ché Guevara, and Titín burst into a Red Army song.

The peasants who were waiting for them at the gate soon began telling the story of how they had taken the farm with help from the MCR (Revolutionary Peasant Movement, the rural equivalent of the MIR), and how two months later (the previous Christmas Eve) the former owners and 150 men had launched a surprise counterattack from the hills, pouring bullets into farm outbuildings for hours and wounding two peasants. Women and children fled, tumbling into the irrigation ditches in the dark.

The government formally expropriated the land and integrated the farm into a regional planning center. Where three farmworkers' families had once lived, there were now 42, mostly Mapuche. They were proud, they said, to be working their own land at last.

left: 1971. A peasant and child wait near the barn at dawn for the day's work assignment.

right: 1971. Titín (back to the camera and knife at waist) gives a pep talk to the assembled Rucalán peasants under a home-made image of Ché on the barn.

Flora (Florentina Alvarez de Troncoso) had never ventured more than ten miles from this farm. She and her husband Julio had 13 children, eight of whom survived. After a lifetime of hard work and subservience, at the age of 59, Flora had become a political activist. She prepared quilts on the barn floor and warm food for the visitors, just as she did for every itinerant organizer who appeared on the farm, and Ted went off with the peasants to photograph them at work.

A year later he was nearby and decided to have another look at the farm. After a futile search for Titín in the city he hired a burly, moustachioed taxi driver to take him to the farm. The driver, who knew how to reach the farm from the correct side of the river, drove directly through the open gate, still overseen by Ché. A few frame houses were rising on the meadow but nobody was in sight. Ted searched for life, finally wandering into the barn where a dozen men hovered in the shadows among the grain sacks.

Where were the campesinos? The men answered that some were working in distant fields, while others had been assigned to nearby farms. They themselves were hoping to participate in house building, but first they had to learn the necessary skills. One said he was a Chilean, and since these Mapuches would not accept him, he was planning to leave. The men, at first shy and at loose ends, became more and more animated as they repeated tales of the old days of combat, of taking and retaking the farm. When the most talkative person stepped into the light his black eye became apparent.

As soon as Flora learned that Ted was back she came running down the hill, discouraged because things were not going well. They sat in her kitchen and talked.

FLORA: I was 18 when I got married. Julio was a widower and my grandmother was old style. She told me she'd rather have me dead than marry a peasant. She hated him, so I was sent away to keep house for a German lady, where I kept everything in perfect order. But I was always crying, always sad, always thinking that if I only had a mother things wouldn't be so bad.

I was standing on that lady's doorstep one day when I saw him coming right toward me. I wanted to run and hide, but he began pleading with me. I got so mixed up that I went to my grandmother, who became so angry she hit me and scratched me with her nails. Then I ran to my aunt.

She said, "The man is a peasant. He's poor, but he's a good worker and he's honest. What else do you want?" She sent for Julio to come to her house and she gave me away, gave me

away like a chicken in the market. No going out, no going steady, no wedding. Nothing! After I had four children he said he'd marry me officially to legitimize them. My grandmother was over a hundred when she died but she never gave me permission to marry.

In the old days, when I heard the boss was coming I'd cry out to the old man, "Run! They want you! Get the animals ready!" And the old man would jump out of bed and go running without shoes. The boss kept pushing, and he kept running. Sometimes at midnight I would still be waiting with the kettle and a pot of food on the fire.

JULIO: They forced us to work days and nights—two days in one. Otherwise it was, "Out to the road with you!" We were never allowed to be free, even on weekends. Sundays didn't exist. Once I heard the story that a family in Puerta Saavedra had pushed its workers into the cauldron where they were boiling potato alcohol. Maybe they just didn't want to pay them.

FLORA: Our family always got very little pay but we knew how to manage. Not one of us had such vices. There are so many drunkards here. Laziness is to blame, not politics. The men don't want to budge, they don't want to work.

Now my son is learning how to drink. I wait up for him, weeping. Every day I tell him he mustn't follow the example of others. But they needle him, "You're not a man if you don't drink." So he drinks and gets drunk and fights. That makes him a real man.

They hold sessions to argue about it, but women have no right to go. Mothers have no rights. The compañeros try to help. They come, they sleep in my house, they get angry, they give advice. First the men deny that they have been drinking, then they promise to behave themselves. Afterward it's the same as it was before. I'm getting old.

The problem is that an organizer comes; after a few hours he goes away; a couple of months later another one appears. They only pass through. I think we must have a compañero watching things every single day.

right: 1972. Julio and Flora in their kitchen.

On a quiet saint's day at the end of 1989, the beginning of the Chilean summer, we set out to rediscover Rucalán. The road from Temuco was edged with sparsely flowering, dusty shrubs, but as we drove west the moisture in the air grew heavier, the dry topaz fields turned to emerald, the pines stretched taller on the hillsides and roses bloomed on the roadside.

An hour later we passed Carahue, the market town founded by Pedro de Valdivia, soon abandoned, and re-established as a river port some three centuries later. Pigs wandered past grimy row houses, and a few young men in satin team jackets hung out in front of their social club. A corpulent priest led a passing procession of celebrants dressed for church. Further on, men in clean field clothes and women wearing aprons were gathering for modest services in a clearing by the road.

The road turned abruptly down a sharp grade onto a jagged rock surface along the smooth Imperial River, whose banks were obscured by willows, yellow loosestrife, Queen Anne's lace as big as a child's head and brilliant blue flowers.

After a dozen shuddering kilometers Ted thought he recognized the steep hill beyond an unmarked driveway, though there was no longer a gate. We drove tentatively past weathered outbuildings on the first plateau, most of which seemed empty, but a dazzling blue Mercedes truck protruded from one. Ché no longer presided over the barn.

Two men who signaled to us from a red farmhouse halfway up the hill turned out to be Juan and Luciano Landarretche, sons of the old owner. They stood with arms akimbo, grimly waiting for us between a car and a pickup truck, both of which displayed the smile stickers of Pinochet's candidate for president.

After some small talk we asked if they might have known Señora Florentina Alvarez, an old woman who had once lived around here. Their impenetrable dark glasses kept us from seeing their eyes as they said they had never heard of her. "Come back in a month, after the election. We have to know the boundaries of the field before we can play the game," they answered when we first asked if we could talk with them a bit.

But Juan seemed to have a change of heart. We thought he might be tempted to try out some of the English he had spoken when he took courses in artificial insemination in Pennsylvania. They appeared to be speaking reluctantly, volunteering nothing, smiling only when they mentioned deaths or disappearances.

JUAN: Our family has been here more than 70 years. We own 4000 acres on Rucalán and some other properties where we grow wheat and raise cattle. For domestic consumption, not for export because, unlike the central valley, we're at the mercy of bad weather, and don't have good access to the transport system.

LUCIANO: You already know what happened. September 8th, 1970 the MIR took our family's farm. They came with machine guns at three in the morning and threw us out in the street. Not a single one of them was from around here. They were all from elsewhere, not even farmers.

JUAN: All the people were from a political movement. None of them could possibly have known how to run this place. They wiped out our family's 30 years of work.

LUCIANO: On December 24th we retook the farm in an armed confrontation. Yes, there were wounded. Deaths? Officially, no! Actually, two! Two of THEM. We were able to keep the farm only one day before the government put us in jail. They claimed we had acted illegally for taking back our own farm, and kept us in jail for 13 days before the trial. We won, so they had to release us.

JUAN: During the three interim years I was a trucker. Luciano had to stay behind because of the disturbances and couldn't attend the university. When the farm was finally returned to us in 1973, nothing was growing. We lost 300 acres of wheat, and they had sold or eaten a thousand head of cattle. None of our original workers took part in the toma and many of them returned to us when we got the farm back. Unfortunately, because of mechanization, we can now use only 18 of them. These past 16 years have been the most prosperous we have ever known.

LUCIANO: There was a permanent party here, a guerrilla camp with guns and Cubans. Even as late as 1977 a couple of outsiders from the MIR were discovered still hanging around. They were soon 'disappeared.'

right: 1989. Luciano and Juan Landarretche in the rose garden of the house overlooking the Imperial River that they built for their mother. The road and the full width of the river are not visible from her hilltop.

Juan made a telephone call and then invited us to meet their mother. The prosperity of the military years became evident when we followed their truck from the rather modest farmhouse in which they had grown up to the lavish contemporary home they said they had built for her.

A small citified woman with a ring of keys at the waist of her tea apron waited at the head of a long drive edged with scores of spindly new rhododendrons. She came forward to greet us in impeccable English, learned from "two maiden ladies and a single gentleman imported from England" by the Temuco gentry when she was a girl. She said she spent her days tending the roses which overlooked the river or expanding the unfinished rock garden which stretched behind the house. Whenever we mentioned the farm or Flora she parried with an abrupt and chatty change of subject, speaking in great detail of studying English, her grand-children, dreams of travel to distant places which had been ended by widowhood.

After leaving the Landarretches, we called on Waldo Cueto, the head of the Committee of Solidarity, the human rights affiliate of the Temuco diocese of the Catholic church, to ask him if he thought their hints of deaths and disappearances had been idle boasting, or if they might have been telling the truth.

WALDO CUETO: We have had no reports of deaths or disappearances in the area of Rucalán, but that is not to say they didn't occur, particularly if the victims were unknown locally. As for the violence involved in taking and retaking farms, we know that people were seriously wounded, but we cannot be absolutely certain that deaths occurred. We suspected some, but could not confirm if those people had been killed, or had simply moved on.

It was certainly true that young men—including the sons of influential families—harassed, attacked and probably killed many people. Running around at night with "Fatherland and Liberty" street gangs was a form of entertainment. During the night you would hear shots from the street, and the next morning read in your newspaper that someone had died in a confrontation. But it was not a confrontation. It was an assassination.

To date, 14 disappearances have been documented in this district. We are certain of ten more, but nobody has come forward to file missing persons claims for those people. Among the known casualties were doctors and teachers. Others were simply working people, like woodcutters. Many of those who suffered had nothing to do with politics, but were simply overheard talking, as we are talking now, and then denounced.

One awful case involved brothers—common thieves known as "los perros" [dogs]—because they stole livestock and ate it. Unfortunately for them, one of their victims was a sergeant in the national police, not a good person to have angered.

They were arrested on a Thursday. On Saturday morning townspeople saw a military truck pull up to the jail, and later drive away towards the Andes carrying 'los perros' and six political prisoners. In the evening the truck returned, carrying only soldiers.

In another case, the government claimed to have unearthed a guerrilla school in the woods. Instead, it turned out that the military had arrested and shot 11 people, whose bodies they then threw into a river, high in the mountains. The story filtered out only because one of the conscripts became very upset and told his family. Later, two of the bodies were found.

right: 1989. The Landarretches and their mother behind her house.

In 1991, more than a year after meeting the Landarretches, we traveled south again. By this time more had been learned about killings and disappearances. From the extensive files of human rights researchers we learned how the Landarretche father and sons, with nine of their friends (far fewer than the gang of 150 described in the peasants' dramatic saga) had attacked the farm with guns on Christmas Eve, wounded Ricardo Mora and Francisco Pilquinao, were charged with attempted murder and eventually acquitted by the court.

This time we carried a letter of introduction to a village schoolmaster who had been in the area during the entire period, and were accompanied by a young man who was documenting human rights abuses and a young woman who was rediscovering the birthplace she had left at the age of six, when her father was murdered in the aftermath of the coup and her mother fled into exile with the children.

Our previous visit had been at year's end, when the entire countryside was in bloom. Now the only color was in yellow lines of "pica-pica" (itch-itch), which kept cattle from wandering, and pink plastic bags of potatoes awaiting pickup in the fields. While spiky tracts of agave still thrived, many of the hillsides which had been covered with pines the year before were now brown and bare. A few "rucas"—the A-frame hut of the southern peasant— nestled under isolated windshaped trees, a scent of eucalyptus was carried by the rain, and birds flew everywhere.

We had to maneuver with wild swings to avoid large gaps in the dirt and stones of the rain-damaged road. The only repair crew we encountered was working at the base of the Rucalán driveway. Our destination was Nehuentue, beyond Rucalán, where we found geese wandering in the empty, muddy streets. The women in the schoolhouse shook their heads and said they had never heard of Señor Florencio Hidalgo, but a wagonload of boys on the main road quickly directed us back to the district school of Tranapuente, very close to Rucalán.

Some pupils playing behind the fence in the Tranapuente schoolyard at recess ran to fetch headmaster Hidalgo, who invited us into his office, examined the photographs and sent for a boy— Flora's 13 year-old grandson—who said his grandfather had died and his grandmother now lived on Capri Street in Temuco. Hidalgo said one of the pictured Mapuches had died of alcoholism, but several others lived nearby, including Armando Ailío, the man with the spade.

right: 1971. Armando Ailío, one of the Mapuches who seized Rucalán, waiting for his work assignment.

Following Hidalgo's directions we found the small house of the Ailíos, from which several young women emerged, one carrying a baby. We showed them some pictures and one of the girls yelled, "That's my pop!" Carmela Huentimilla, Armando's wife, padded out quietly. "I was watching from the window and recognized you," she told Ted.

Carmela recalled that the old days when they worked the farm for themselves had been very good days indeed. They had shared the communal land and responsibility for wheat, potatoes and petit-pois. Each family also cultivated its personal plot. The farm had been too poor to support the six cows which were there when they took over, so they sold them. (The Landarretches had complained of losing a thousand head of cattle.)

Carmela recalled that after the coup the young and old land-lords accompanied police who came to retake the farm with guns and grenades. When the Mapuches left quietly they had no excuse to use their arms. Now the Ailío family owns no land; instead they pay rent and work for others, barely surviving. But Carmela says, "I give my love to all, without judging."

Armando was at work on a distant farm. There was no way to know how late he would return so we stood around in the drizzle, trying to figure out what to do. As we talked, he came striding over the hill swinging a walking stick, walked up very close to Ted and stared uncertainly, until Ted asked, "Don't you remember me?" Armando stumbled forward to hug him.

He described a night before his arrest when he and other peasants watched as big landowners and high military officers from all over the district flocked to the Landarretche house for a grand party celebrating the death of Allende. (Human rights investigators later expressed interest in the guests because some of the names had appeared in reports of violations.)

Armando and two others were sent to prison for six years, where he said he had been starved but not beaten, although some others were treated very badly. How had the family survived while he was gone? "We begged on the streets," Carmela said.

Chile's return to democracy has not affected them much. Life in general is not so different from what it was during the military years. Armando thinks that perhaps some day it will be better. "They won," he said. "And we lost."

right: 1991. Armando Ailío and Carmela Huentimilla with one of their daughters.

Most of our last day in Temuco was spent searching for Flora, knocking at doors of little row houses and grocery stores on Capri Street, where her grandson had said she lived. We exhausted every possibility before taking one last chance on the muddy tract beyond the paved road. There we found her.

She was living with her daughter Maria, who had become a permanent squatter there after joining a land seizure three years earlier. Maria had been a girl when Ted first saw her at Rucalán. Now she was a 40 year-old widow, selling used clothing in the open air market by the railway station.

The single layer of boards on their house was not tight against the cold damp climate of Temuco but the main room had a wood floor, a metal stove and a cooking range. Neatly lined-up narrow iron beds completely filled an adjoining room. In the yard were a vegetable garden, a dog, some scratching chickens, a large white rabbit and the kitchen sink, filled by a hose and draining directly onto the ground.

We had interrupted the women as they were preparing wheat hominy at the sink. Leaving the work half-done they rushed inside, moved the crude table into the center of the room, spread a clean white cloth, and began to boil coffee and fry great quantities of eggs. Flora had always said one showed love by serving food and drink.

When it was time to depart for our flight to Santiago, Flora tried to press the white rabbit upon us to bring home, claiming that it had not been raised for food or cash, although we knew it must have been. We promised to look down from the plane, which always flew directly overhead from the nearby airport, and they said they would be standing there, waving their final goodbye.

FLORA: Today I had a feeling I would receive an embrace from far away, but I thought it would be my grandson. I never thought to see you again.

You remember the farm and how production increased at first? It was terrific. But the drinking made things worse, perhaps because it was the first time the peasants ever had a bit of cash to spend. The last straw was when a drunk turned over a tractor.

When the military came they brought times of fear and hatred. I'm not surprised that the Landarretches deny that they knew me. It may have been 'inconvenient' for them to remember me, but I remember them very well. The mother always used to come to our place to swim because we lived in such a good spot on the river.

After the coup the military came looking for my sons and

caught two of them. Later they were released, but a couple of other young men who were badly beaten did not survive. We heard that Titín was sheltered by the Bishop of Temuco.

Soldiers came to raid my house, looking for arms. Of course we had none. They hadn't expected to find any, but all the same they destroyed all our possessions for amusement. They even took away the picture of Julio and me that you sent to us.

None of us were permitted to stay there. People went anyplace where they thought they might be accepted, though most of us tried to remain in the area if we could possibly do so. Our family became "allegados"—people who are given permission to remain on a piece of land by those who own it. In our case we were taken in by a Mapuche community.

After Julio died Maria promised me that once she had her own home I must come to live with her. I've been here only three months. At 79 years of age I find it very difficult to become adjusted to city life, but with an old-age pension of $70 a year there is no place for me in the countryside. So now I am an "allegado" here.

right: Temuco, 1991. Flora and her daughter Maria in Maria's house in a Temuco squatter settlement. Before moving there Flora had never ventured more than ten miles from her birthplace.

A migrant laborer who walked the roads from farm to farm with a sack on his shoulder was called "afuerino" (outsider). "Afuerino is not a beautiful word. What kind of name is that for a man?" asked one. Eight afuerinos, led by José Sepúlveda Cabezas, met Allende, his daughter Beatriz and the Minister of Agriculture in 1971. The following is from their interview.

SEPULVEDA: Comrade President Doctor: We came to tell you our problems. Farms are passing into the agrarian reform but we still have no place. Not that we're looking for land, it's permanent work we want. Food and a space of our own, so we don't have to sleep in the straw or under a bridge or a tree.

When we pass through a city the police give us a hard time. They go through the trifling possessions in our sacks, keep us overnight and force us to do unpaid labor. In the country it's the same. This has all happened to me.

If we must walk a long time to find work, people look at us as if we come from another planet. It's shameful that we must do this when there is so much land to work in our Chile.

We don't have proper papers so we can't get decent medical care. If we get sick we treat ourselves with country herbs. If an afuerino has no work, others will share what they have. We're just as capable of humanitarian instincts as highly educated persons.

An afuerino is destined never to have a mate. How can she walk with us through terrible hills in search of work? A woman gets weary; she cannot become accustomed to this life, so we must live forever as bachelors and die without knowing love.

ALLENDE: We have an obligation, not only a human but a social obligation, to seek a solution. But solutions cannot be found all at once, you understand?

SEPULVEDA: Yes, all too well.

above: The Talca jail, 1972. While the government was negotiating the transfer of El Marco, the afuerinos ate one of the owner's cows. José Sepúlveda Cabezas, the leader who agreed to accept responsibility for their act, served a two month sentence.

right: 1972. Afuerino José Záldivar is 46 years old.

Not far from Talca was El Marco, owned by a businessman in the city: 150 acres of pasture and potatoes, six houses, a few sheds, a barn and 15 animals. Five months after Allende said the problem could not be solved overnight, 30 men seized El Marco, renaming it "The First Triumph of the Afuerinos." Summarily evicted by a government official and a squad of police, the men slept in the woods for nine nights. Sepúlveda appealed to the Minister of Agriculture, who then stepped in to legalize their claim on the grounds that the farm had been underutilized.

The government set compensation for the farm's owner and ordered the afuerinos to return his animals. A production plan was developed, calling for subsistence wages, credits from the state bank, and switching from potatoes to wheat.

When word got around, afuerinos showed up from everywhere. The acreage was too small to support them all, so there were more land seizures. At the third one, an armed gang of ultra-rightist youths from Fatherland and Liberty surprised the squatters in their sleep, tied them up, pistol-whipped them, threw them into trucks and dumped them on a distant road. The brutality of the raid created great sympathy for giving them the land, even from people who had argued against undisciplined land grabs.

At El Marco the men walked with their scythes for almost an hour to chop and burn brush before planting the wheat. Each person took his turn as cook, but there were few plates, so some men had to spoon their food from the common pot. They boiled water from a nearby irrigation ditch for drinking. At night they bathed in the same ditch. All of them had been shocked by two long-haired Argentinian journalists who stayed with them. "They never once took a bath."

René had become a migrant at the age of 14 when, after a day of loading wheat onto trucks, the boss tossed handfuls of farina at the peasants for them to cook. René got angry and threw his ration against the office wall; his family was thrown out. He heard about the farm on the radio and found the men in the woods where they were hiding out. "After the elections," he recalled, "whenever we went to the rich people for work they said, "Go to Allende! Ask him for a job!""

Ramón, one of the organizers, said half the men were illiterate. "There is little to do at night. Pitch coins, talk. Play cards, talk. Sometimes on Saturday nights we walk three miles to the bus to take in a movie in Talca. Mostly, it's the land, the sky and us. Afuerinos used to steal from one another, even their sacks. Now the spirit is beautiful. We eat together, work together, sleep together. There are arguments, but every day our fellowship grows."

Onofrio added, "Day by day we're changing our character." But one fellow was skeptical. "We work like slaves for very little pay. I can go to sleep and not wake up in the morning. Why should I think of the future?"

right: 1972. The afuerinos make up straw beds on the cement floor of the barn, cook over an open fire, eat from the common pot, drink from and wash in an irrigation ditch.

above: 1972. Afuerinos on the antenna which is still there in 1991.

right: 1991. Farm manager Luís Homero Melendez in front of the barn where afuerinos once ate and slept. Melendez grew up on El Marco and his entire family is dependent on the owner. He has called the city and received instructions to get rid of us.

When we started looking for them in 1991 we heard that a quarter of a million afuerinos no longer existed, and their places as temporary farmhands are now likely to be taken by housewives, students and the underemployed. Accompanied by rural organizers, each with his own story of prison or exile, we drove hundreds of kilometers on dirt roads and talked to dozens of men and women in four towns, but we found not one afuerino. A trail which began at the National Peasant Federation in Talca eventually provided us with a couple of contradictory stories, but we never learned what had really happened.

One person described the owners of El Marco. "The Zarors were like Godfathers, and still are." We visited Don Carlos Zaror's rice mill in Talca. He would not see us, but assigned the job to his chief engineer, who related this story: The afuerinos who took El Marco were actually political activists, not farmers; they ate all the animals, for which nobody was ever punished; instead of cultivating the land they sold it for a profit.

He drew a map of the circuitous route to the farm, which we might not otherwise have found. Then he asked us to send some growth hormone from the U. S. to help his undersized daughter.

El Marco looked the same, perhaps messier, littered with trash, pigs and somnolent dogs. Small dirty children peered from behind a broken-down wagon and timid men sneaked looks at us around corners. Foreman Luís Homero Melendez, who said he had grown up on El Marco and worked there before and after the toma, telephoned a second Zaror brother in the city for instructions when we asked about photographs. He was told to throw us out.

Each person we visited sent us to another who might know more. On our last evening in the area we met Carlos Sepúlveda (unrelated to José), a large handsome old man with huge peasant hands and peasant speech. It turned out that he had known the farm well and sympathized with the afuerinos because in his youth he had worked for many different owners.

He said their first year had been rocky because they were so inexperienced at running things. By the second year they had learned enough to expand their crops and brought in an amazing rice harvest. Sepúlveda said they had made the transition from afuerino to peasant before the military dispersed them. Lacking local roots, they disappeared, and everything went back to where it had been a half century before.

When we got home we tried to keep our bargain with Zaror's engineer, but an expert on growth hormone said the drug was too dangerous to dispense by mail order.

In the Mills and Mines

The Chilean labor movement began in the nitrate pits of the arid north, where the world's only supply of the gray crystals that yield both fertilizer and explosives covers some 450 miles of the Atacama Desert. Although Chile had won the territory from its northern neighbors in a bloody four-year war at the end of the 19th century, the nitrates for which Europe hungered belonged mainly to the British. Instead of re-investing their royalties, the Chilean gentry built mansions in frontier towns and imported vast quantities of perfume and champagne. Foreigners became so powerful that they could finance the overthrow of presidents.

The men who processed nitrates in the scorching desert by boiling it in open pits were paid in scrip, and compelled to shop in the company store. Prostitutes abounded in the mining camps, while drinking water was scarce. Miners died young.

A grisly event in 1907 fueled song and legend and helped establish Chile's combative and highly politicized labor tradition. To protest the brutal working conditions, thousands of miners trudged on foot to the port of Iquique where, reassured by the presence of warships in the harbor, they stood patiently in a schoolyard, waiting for the government to intervene on their behalf. Instead, troops were ordered to fire, and wagons hauled away the corpses after dark for interment in mass graves. The number of dead, many of them single men who were never reported missing, is unknown. Estimates range from hundreds to thousands.

Germany developed synthetic nitrates after World War I. Chile's nitrate boom collapsed and the economy, dependent on nitrate exports, went into a tailspin. When copper became the dominant export, the British were replaced by Americans— Grace, Guggenheim, Kennecott and Anaconda. The historic pattern of foreign exploitation of the country's natural riches continued.

When printer Luis Emilio Recabarren was elected to the congress in 1906 he was barred from his seat after refusing to take an oath. Nevertheless, as the "father" of the labor movement, he remained immensely popular. Later he founded the Worker's Socialist Party, the forerunner of the Communists.

Clotario Blest was a charismatic, romantic revolutionary of the Christian Left who sympathized with the MIR and was critical of the Communists and the Socialists. Friend and enemy alike called him by his first name. During the dictatorship, even Pinochet did not touch Clotario.

CLOTARIO, 1972: This government is full of promise, but people follow coldly, without spontaneity. There are men in the government from the parties of the left who preach revolution, but still live in big houses and enjoy excessive creature comforts. The workers have been deceived so many times that they don't believe any politicians.

Let's have no illusions. The right lies and it conspires against the people. They fear nothing and they respect nothing. When somebody in misery asks for bread, they give them bullets or prison instead. Now that there's all this talk of legalism and constitutionality, our government must watch out for attacks by its proponents, and not play their game. We're only in the waiting room of the revolution, and that is a situation that's sure to end in confrontation—between the people on one side and the exploiters on the other.

The big parties like the Communists and Socialists are only interested in gaining members; it's the MIR that deals with workers' real problems, real desires, and creates a sense of participation, of mystical fervor.

Revolutions are not made "en frio" [coldly], but with "rojo vivo" [living red or hot blood]. The idea may be in the head, but it is also in the heart. And what is in the heart is the most important because it is love, not reason, that drives the world. We must live what we preach, and thereby touch the hearts of men.

right: Santiago, 1972. May Day. Clotario stands for Allende's salute and applause at a huge outdoor rally. Among the dignitaries on the platform is Cardinal Raúl Silva Henriquez, under whose leadership the Catholic church established the Vicariate of Solidarity to protect human rights and support the victims of repression.

Clotario, who had been a small boy at the time of the Iquique massacre, began organizing in his youth. That was a time when unions were disguised as cultural or sports clubs. In 1953 he became the first president of the CUT (Central Workers Union), from which he resigned eight years later to protest what he considered its waning militancy and its subservience to the orthodox political parties.

In 1972, the wiry Clotario, dressed in denim because, "I want to be a worker not only in my soul, but on the outside," welcomed visitors into his dark study where books and papers were piled up everywhere. The walls were covered by posters and photographs, including Recabarren and a martyred Colombian priest. Roaming freely on his papers was Gato (simply cat). He also introduced a great, plodding dog. "I call him Momio (reactionary) because he doesn't work, but merely eats and gets fat."

In 1989 everyone in Santiago seemed to know Clotario's health had failed. He reportedly had lost the will to live until he was moved from a hospital to the Franciscan monastery. There we found the frail, elegant old man in dressing gown and pajamas, sitting outside his spartan bedroom. Other rooms off the long, windowed arcade overlooking neglected gardens seemed empty. Keeping Clotario company were a nurse, a student with a guitar and a monk in work clothes.

Clotario's face brightened at the sight of guests. He called for tea, but by the time he reached the plank table on the arm of the monk, he had forgotten about us and retreated into confusion.

A newspaper soon featured a Christmas scene in full color, with glowing tree and happy children surrounding Clotario, who stood stiffly in cardboard-new, electric blue denims. The monk in brown, sashed habit stood watchfully off to one side. "I'm very content with this new life of peace and spirituality," Clotario was reputed to have said. Some days later he died.

left: Santiago, 1972. Clotario Blest at home with his dog Momio and cat Gato.

right: 1989. Clotario sits outside his bedroom in the Franciscan monastery shortly before his death.

In the early 1970s we also came to know Oscar Ibáñez, a labor organizer who exemplified a different strain in the Chilean unions. Not romantic but practical, not saintly but stolid, a loyalist more than an individualist.

In 1943 Oscar had come to Yarur, the country's largest textile plant, as soccer coach, doubling on the night shift as a weaver. The powerful Yarur family also owned a large bank and a powerful radio network. If you had a job there in those days the company was your life. Old Juan Yarur expected his employees to pledge their fealty by signing his book and swearing before a human skull and a crucifix.

A worker who spied on someone suspected of being a 'red' would get lighter work and occasional meals in the white-collar cafeteria, while the disloyal worker might be held incommunicado in the factory by Yarur's armed security guard. When the factory was expropriated in 1971 the union found suspects' names listed in reports of the "Vigilance and Security Committee."

Oscar was identified as a union militant and fired after six months. Only later did he join the Communist Party. When the plant was expropriated 28 years after his tenure there, he was appointed one of three government managers.

left: Yarur, 1972. Workers had been expected to inscribe their names in the owner's book and swear their personal loyalty before the skull and crucifix. These articles are still on display as a reminder of how things once were.

right: Santiago, May Day, 1972. A year after expropriation, manager Oscar Ibáñez (moustache and hat) marches with plant workers and union officers under the banner, "Yarur, Territory Free of Exploitation." Marching with them is Oscar Garretón (dark beard and vest), Assistant Minister of the Economy, whose responsibilities include the textile industry.

above: Bank of Chile, Santiago, 1971. Major industries were nationalized but Chile's largest private financial institution remains private. Some of Allende's most vehement critics sit on its board of directors. Jorge Fontaine (in light suit), taking a cue from Sen. Joseph McCarthy, issued his own list of subversives to boycott in the business world. Javier Vial (second from right) is known as a "piranha." (In the military years he amassed both vast debt and a vast fortune. The mismanaged bank was finally nationalized by Pinochet—to bail it out.)

right: Ex-Yarur, 1972. After nationalization the board of directors of the textile plant consisted of professionals, government managers, workers and union leaders. Ibáñez is seated at left.

Oscar Ibáñez sat in the old executive offices, not quite comfortable behind the bosses' massive desk, although he had made a self-conscious effort to look respectable by putting a suit jacket on his bulky frame.

OSCAR: The first step is to help develop the workers' mentality, to bring them to a higher stage of consciousness. We have to fight capitalist notions of individualism, egoism and selfishness. But they're not going to change overnight. It's a step-by-step process.

The Chilean process is without precedent. We're creating new forms while retaining bourgeois legality. Workers here are learning discipline by taking part in directing their factory. Their participation isn't formal, it's real. They know it's theirs and they will defend it, but the contradictions have not yet reached the stage of confrontation. First we want to take advantage of all existing means to disarm the capitalists. We want to fight on our own terms, not the enemy's.

The young people of the MIR want confrontation now. I can't accept it when they attack us Communists as bourgeois and non-revolutionary. We've fought for years. We've suffered repression. The working class has been dying for a hundred years to reach this juncture and the MIR wants to throw it away in three days of fighting.

They think armed struggle is the only road to power. Arms may be necessary for revolution but they will always find their way into the hands of revolutionaries. The important thing is the development of ideology and consciousness, the willingness to sacrifice one's life. And that takes a little longer.

right: Yarur, 1972. Oscar Ibáñez dances the cueca (Chile's national dance) with Congresswoman Mireya Baltra, while Assistant Minister of the Economy Oscar Garretón plays the guitar during a week long celebration of the first anniversary of nationalization.

The national textile union helped us locate Oscar again in 1989. Their organization had been declared illegal, its building and records seized numerous times, but they kept reorganizing. Oscar lived in a gritty working class neighborhood. He was having a hard time financially but he hoped Aylwin's election would make it possible to find work. In 1973 he was caught and tortured. When he could not work, he sold his house and bought a pharmacy. Then the DINA raided it, the bank took away his credit, he was denounced to the Ministry of Health, and lost the business.

After that he sold electrical supplies, but that ended because plainclothesmen would harass the customers. He sold underwear door-to-door and in the street. He was a weaver in a small company that failed. Oscar says his perspective is still the same: the worker is forever pitted against the boss.

After many years Mireya Baltra, his dance partner at the celebration, returned from foreign exile and was elected to the Senate. Assistant Minister of the Economy Garretón again became an important public figure. Oscar was unemployed.

OSCAR IBANEZ: When troops surrounded the factory we didn't resist; there was nothing with which to resist. People just threw themselves on the floor. When they transported us to the garrison of the anti-guerrilla regiment they told us we'd better not move. But I fell. I put my hands over my head so they broke my fingers with a rifle butt (he showed a misshapen hand). Black Berets [the Chilean equivalent of Green Berets, U.S. trained in Panama] were everywhere. On the spot they killed a MIRista. Put him in a truck, two shots, then drove away.

Next day they took us to Chile Stadium with our heads in our laps. One man raised his head and they shot him. They took our belts and stole our rings and watches. Up in the stands soldiers with machine guns kept cocking them and clicking the bolts all night long. One prisoner threw himself off the third deck. For some reason an officer got angry with one man, threw him on the ground, put his foot on the fellow's chest and told a soldier to give him his rifle. Then he smashed the fellow's head with it and blood and brains went flying everywhere. I think I survived because I said I was just one of the office employees. When they asked others "Who is this guy?" they said the same.

Then they took me to the smaller National Stadium where I was with 80 others in a locker room. We slept on the floor, on a toilet seat, and two or three curled up in the shower. We were somewhat ready for the torturers when they came because we'd been talking, convincing ourselves that we knew nothing. A psychology professor showed us techniques to help blot out memory.

So it was no surprise. They put a hood on me, hit me, made me walk barefoot on rocks. The blows never stopped. I still have scars on my legs. Even my father never hit me so much (he laughs). They asked if I had stolen the relics from old Yarur's office. Probably soldiers took them.

I normally weighed 75 kilos but when I got out after six weeks I weighed 50. They trashed my house and left my wife crying. Soldiers hung around outside. They pursued me everywhere. My presence was compromising my family so I began six months of clandestine life. Being underground even cut me off from going to the church or the human rights people for help.

After they ruined my pharmacy they arrested me again on fake weapons charges. Fortunately, the prosecutor had been at law school with my lawyer. He called me in. "Mr. Ibáñez, you are a serious man. Unfortunately you are also a Communist, though you may be one who believes in the parliamentary system. I do not believe you will take up a gun, so I am going to free you. But I don't want to see you ever again. If I do, your luck is surely going to change."

It's going to take another generation to heal the trauma. I can never forget my friends who were killed. We have to look to the future, so let's pardon the guilty—but only after we identify each and every one of them. Why not pick up a machine gun and shoot them all? I feel I could easily do it. Why not join the Manuel Rodriguez Patriotic Front (the armed wing of the Communists that was responsible for the 1986 attempt on Pinochet's life)? Because the truth is that we now need a philosophy of life, not of death.

The dictatorship is going away. Now it's like we're still in a box, but the box is gradually getting bigger and there is more space.

right: Santiago, 1989. Oscar outside his house.

After the coup the face of Oscar Garretón, a leader of the MAPU (Movement for Popular Action) and Allende's Assistant Minister of the Economy, responsible for the textile industry, was prominently displayed on wanted posters. A reward was offered for turning him in. He found refuge as a professor in Colombia, but when the long arm of the junta reached into Argentina to kill ex-Gen. Prats and his wife, Garretón no longer felt safe. He went to Cuba, where he found time to reflect.

Later he worked in foreign trade in Argentina, where he also conducted a radio program. In 1987 he got permission to enter Chile for 30 days to visit his dying father. His father recovered instead, and Garretón announced to the Ministry of the Interior that he would not leave. They told him that if he stayed he would go to jail, which he did.

He remained there until the plebiscite. When Aylwin became president he was appointed chief of the Santiago Metro, arguably the best subway system in Latin America, certainly the cleanest.

At the same time he runs the transportation system he must travel once a month to sign in at the prison as a condition of his parole, and a 1973 sedition charge has not yet been wiped out. "So goes the transition," he said. "A bit of surrealism."

OSCAR GARRETON: They didn't torture me, although the Valparaíso prison is pretty awful. It was payment for being allowed back into the country, but it was also a post-graduate education because I was able to study the entire Chilean economy. I had visitors, exercised every day, and we organized soccer matches in which even the guards played. I was in much better shape than I am now. I gave classes in economics. At first both guards and prisoners were suspicious of my motives, but we came to respect one another.

We began discussions—both exiles and people inside Chile—on the form that resistance against the dictatorship should take, calling it "reconstructing the popular world," as opposed to the tendency of militants of the more heroic parties to butt their heads against a very tough state, sometimes getting them broken in the process. Instead of militant action, we placed the greatest value on soup kitchens, theatre groups, religious masses.

We came to question the Leninist concept of a vanguard party at the peak of the pyramid, with all those at the bottom consigned to lesser importance. We came to treasure the contributions of the church; the importance of pluralism; the participation of all, not just the left or the ideologically committed. And we rejected the use of arms, for in the armed struggle the savior must be the Party, since the people never have any weapons.

When the junta opened voter registration we leaped for joy. Some people in the left believed it was a setup, that the dictatorship would never allow an election it might lose.

We've changed a great deal. And I'm happy that we've changed. The worst thing would have been to remain trapped in time while the world changed around us. If we had remained nostalgic for the past, we might have turned into the reactionary left, condemned to crying for the good old days and singing the same old songs.

left: September, 1973. Garretón (in circle) on the front-page wanted poster that also targeted Mickey of New Havana.

right: Santiago, 1991. Here Oscar Garretón and an assistant are taking a ride on the Santiago Metro.

General Augusto Pinochet's career was launched in a region of Chile where he may be most hated. During a 25-day strike in 1947 he was an eager young officer whose troops broke into miners' homes, dragging them back to work or to jail.

The coal deposits that snake for miles under the Pacific Ocean south of Concepción were originally purchased from Araucano chiefs for 150 pesos in 1837. Coal dug from poorly-ventilated shafts by naked miners was hauled out by horses kept in the tunnels for months at a time. As mechanization progressed the miners who were displaced by machines eked out a living as fishermen or "chinchorerros," combing slag piles for bits of coal to sell.

The coal miners struck again in 1960, this time against a wage freeze proposed by a U.S. advisory commission and vigorously promoted by then-President Jorge Alessandri. The strikers adopted tactics from the famous 1912 Lawrence, Massachusetts textile strike. Their community soup kitchens functioned for three months, even through earthquake; food and clothing came by ship from distant places; children were shipped to other cities to publicize their plight and save them from cold and hunger. The strike culminated in a march of thirty thousand men, women and children, all wearing their Sunday best.

The wage freeze was broken, but it was not until 1967 that they won the eight-hour day and portal-to-portal pay for the long underground trip to the coal seams.

Alessandri tried to campaign in Lota when he ran for president again in 1970 as the candidate of the conservative National Party. Everywhere he turned the streets were blockaded against him and he left without making a single speech. After Allende took office he came to the Lota plaza to announce the nationalization of the mines. Many of the old coal miners wept.

Pinochet did not forget Lota. Immediately after the coup the mayor and three top officials of the mine union were shot. (The son of one of them was in prison for trying to kill Pinochet 13 years later.) The union was trying to rebuild its smashed headquarters, as well as its membership, but only 4,000 miners were needed to do the work of 14,000.

right: Lota, 1972. Miners and their sons emerge from the tunnels after a day of voluntary labor.

In summer the road to Lota proceeds past busy beaches and hostelries. The first distant views of the town show green hills and then bright flowering shrubs that seem to be tumbling down the slopes. But the final closeup reveals the real Lota, with its steep unpaved roads, twisting switchbacks, grim tenements and bleak downtown, all of it covered by dust. It is a place that has remained untouched by Chile's economic miracle.

The rebellious inhabitants of Lota, undaunted by the miserable community of slums and saloons, were passionately involved in politics, supporting Allende almost unanimously. Pinochet took his revenge, and then modernization took its toll. When fewer miners were needed to bring up coal, the mine's military managers got their chance to get rid of troublemakers. While Chile's army of jobless men cleaned streets and beautified parks in other cities, Lota was frozen out. The town became grayer, poorer and meaner.

right: The characteristic Lota tenements remain unchanged.

Omar Sanhueza, a fluent orator, was head of the Lota industrial union in the days of a benevolent government. His older brother had been killed in the 1947 strike. After a day of volunteer work in the mines in 1972 Omar said, "We're trying to overcome, to transcend ourselves. We have to make sacrifices if we want this government to survive. Money, it's beautiful, but voluntary labor exalts us, and that has no price."

In 1973 troops occupied the union's giant cultural center. When they were through with it, they smashed it up. Miners went to jail or were driven into exile. For a little while Omar evaded capture, but they caught him and sent him to a concentration camp for a year. When he got out he submerged in Santiago for 15 clandestine years, evading re-arrest by moving often and working at off-the-books jobs.

Anticipating the end of the blacklist after the new president was elected, Omar returned home to ask for a job (any job) in the mines. We found him in Lota on the day management gave him his answer. Since they were still military holdovers, it came as no surprise that they turned him down.

When we received permission to enter the mine property with our assistants, guards had no way of knowing that one of them was Omar. Everywhere we walked he was recognized and hailed by excited miners, although at a safe distance. He was confident that he would eventually be rehired.

OMAR, Lota, 1989: During all those years in Santiago people knew me as Julian. If I put together all the jobs I was able to find in that time they wouldn't total three years work. Pinochet has certainly produced the economic miracle of South America. His great invention is Minimum Employment. It does away with unemployment. First, you kill people outright, then you kill the rest bit-by-bit, by paying them so little that they starve.

My youngest daughter was only two years-old when I left home. We met recently for the first time in these 15 years but first I sent her a tape telling her about myself, and why it was that I had to be away from her for so long. When we met at last we cried like children.

above: Lota, 1972. Omar Sanhueza has just finished a day of voluntary coal digging.

right: Lota, 1989. Omar stands in the smashed cultural center. Birds swoop through rusted roof trusses, past faded murals and slogans. Weeds sprout through rubble-strewn cement floors, the twisted window frames in his modest old office hold only shards. So far the union has been able to rehabilitate only a windowless office and small dental clinic.

above: Lota, 1971. The Manriquez family has always worked in the mines and been involved in politics, including Pedro (in hard hat) and his son Waldo (bearded), who is proud of working at the dangerous face of the coal.

right: Lota, 1989. None of the Manriquez men work the coal today. Pedro (in plaid shirt) is retired. Waldo (wearing beret) was jailed without being charged or tried. Soldiers regularly beat him into unconsciousness and woke him by urinating on him. One morning, after 14 months, they said "Sorry," told him to keep his nose out of politics and sent him home. Now he drives a delivery van.

We knocked at the door of Milton Gonzalez' row house early in the morning. He and his wife Graciela Faundez were not expecting guests, but the floors and tabletops in the tiny house gleamed. Strong coffee, fresh bread and cheese appeared magically. Milton sat at the table reminiscing over old photographs and what had happened to the people in them, even one despised union man who had gone over to the military and turned in his comrades.

Until the coup, Milton had been head of both the Coronel (companion mine to Lota) Popular Unity and the local Socialist Party. Afterward he was guarded by friends who moved him to a different safe house after each raid. He recalled that when the police took people away in these raids, some of the younger men clamored for counter attacks on the police barracks. They were dissuaded because the only arms any of them possessed were sticks and a couple of ancient Argentinian revolvers.

During two years in prison Milton made tapestries. The first was a single blood-red rose, its thorny stem held by a disembodied hand, and the words, "Love to my wife and children." He worked on the second, his story of the miners, during much of his sentence.

After release, Milton and two friends pooled resources to make willow-twig furniture because they couldn't get jobs. The living room settee is all that remains of that disastrous enterprise. They lost everything, and Milton spent the next four years as an itinerant vendor. Later he went to work for the church human rights organization. Old friends were after him to rejoin the party,

but if he went to a meeting he might lose his job, since the church feared that partisan politics could taint its efforts.

MILTON, 1989: A few months after the coup they called me back to work. It wasn't the company that persecuted me after that, it was the new union leaders appointed by the company. We had worked so hard in the union and in politics, only to become as helpless as a declawed lion.

It was very difficult when some of us from different parties started working together clandestinely. Sometimes we would meet in a home, sometimes in the woods, sometimes on the beach as if we were going swimming. A French priest who tried to help us was deported. We tried to educate people about the dangers of the new decrees, which had finally succeeded in privatizing the mines and invalidating all the benefits we had won in so many years of struggle.

I was arrested on March 10th, 1981, when my wife and children were at home. First 30 soldiers with machine guns surrounded the block. All of this for just one person.

They accused me of directing a guerrilla army and of possessing arms and explosives. Those explosives were really a bit of old mine dynamite one fellow had kept at home.

left: This framed parchment is a devout family's memento of Pope John Paul II's 1982 visit to Chile. It is inscribed to Milton, Graciela and the children for the "occasion of your liberation," an event which had not yet occurred.

far right: Schwager, 1989. Milton Gonzalez and Graciela Faundez at home. Over the sideboard is the tapestry he made in jail, picturing work in the mine, the company tenements, a flaming disaster, a man behind bars, a woman waiting at home, a rainbow, doves flying free and a happy child.

Edmundo Galindo was a strong union man. His wife used to take her babies to meetings and demonstrations. After she died Edmundo brought up the children by himself. We came across Edmundo's youngest son (born well after this photograph) painting Aylwin signs on the sidewalk with some friends. He told us where to find his father.

When Edmundo was thrown out of the mine he found work as a fish processer. Chileans have never been fond of fish, so before the foreigners began to clamor for Chile's oysters, clams, abalone, mussels and sea urchins, nobody mined the sea's rich harvest seriously. We tried to visit Edmundo during his 12-hour shift at the Japanese-owned plant but they turned us away, saying it would be impossible to see him, even for a few moments.

right: Lota, 1972. The Galindo family at home.

When General Pinochet designed the 1988 plebiscite to transform himself from dictator to president, fear still pervaded Chile and it seemed unlikely that he could lose. But in the privacy of the voting booth Chileans dealt him a mortal blow. As soon as his rejection became known, there was a spontaneous rush to the streets, where people danced and embraced strangers. Those who had marked "NO" on their ballots described a universal reaction: the joy of suddenly feeling unafraid.

Prevented from running himself, Pinochet anointed civilian Hernán Büchi, who had served in his cabinet, as the preferred candidate of the military. The modishly-coiffed Büchi, in skimpy jogging shorts or striding with jacket nonchalantly flung over one shoulder, projected a youthful image compared with 71 year-old Patricio Aylwin, candidate of the unified opposition.

On the last campaign weekend a million Aylwin supporters, one-third of Santiago's population, gathered in a park. Buchi's last rally occurred during rush hour on the city's busiest downtown plaza, where enthusiastic partisans mixed with hordes of office workers who were trapped on their way home.

One demonstrator asserted, "Buchi's the one who'll bring a stable future." Another said, "There were disappearances on both sides. They go away, then after a year turn up again. You forget what we suffered under Allende." A fellow peddling Büchi banners confessed, "You want the truth? I'm here because I'm unemployed." He was proud that he had sold nothing at Aylwin's rally. "There I was a participant."

Afterward, prep school students stuffed themselves into cars and sped through wealthy zones of the city, tooting Buchi's tune on their horns. By election eve, emboldened Aylwin backers, predicting Pinochet's fate, responded with their own rhythm, "He's going to fall."

The morning after Aylwin's victory Verónica, our sleek tanned landlady told us, "I don't just feel bad. I'm sick. The Allende years were terrible. If you were for the government they'd give you a card to buy milk. We wanted the coup. It was wonderful. I don't know anyone who was tortured. Those people who were killed were asking for it. I know Büchi personally. I can't even stand looking at Aylwin on TV. He has a liar's face. I can see he's lying now."

A travel agent from a solid right-wing family—not well-off but very well-connected—said, "It was a tough government that punished people when they defied our good customs. I never had trouble with the military because I don't wear a gun and I don't assault banks. Democracy? I don't know if democracy is the best system. It's a good system for clean people."

above left: In the contest of campaign posters Aylwin was the clear winner. His detractors mostly hired people to rip posters from the walls, while many of his backers found more ingenious ways to distort Buchi's image. Inspired by the campaign slogan, "Büchi is different," one voter's overpainting sends its own message.

right: A Büchi supporter preens herself at his final election rally.

111

Patricio Aylwin, Chile's 73 year-old lame-duck president, an opposition leader in the days of the Popular Unity, earned the enmity of the military and its allies for his criticism of Pinochet's harsh rule. But the respect in which he was held by the population, even those who were critical of the slow pace of justice and social reform, was unmistakable.

After his victory by absolute majority in a three-man race, the courtly Aylwin's popularity continued unabated, in part because he presided over an improving economy, in part because he reined in the military, in part because he worked to heal the wounded country. His four-year transition from tyranny to democracy was scheduled to end in 1994 with the resumption of the traditional six-year presidency.

above: Santiago, 1989. At the final Aylwin rally a large banner reads, "For a Decent Chile, Aylwin for President." This theme recurred often among a populace wearied by years of pain and fear, craving time to recover its health.

right: Santiago, 1991. While the country remains largely indifferent, bitterness lingers over the fate of a small number of the dictatorship's prisoners who remain in jail. Their families and a network of supporters continue to press for their release, among them these students who depict Aylwin as a puppet of the military and ask "Who's in charge? What happened to the Rettig report?" Ironically, at the same moment, the president is addressing the May Day rally a few hundred yards away.

Thanks to its exports of copper, iron, gold and silver, fish meal, wood, wine and fruit, Chile is doing pretty well. The 1991 rate of inflation was a manageable 18.7%, while productivity, employment and wages kept inching up.

The whittling of prices for exports and the increasing costs of imports may be a warning sign for the future, but for now things look good, although many people worry about the selling-off of the country's natural bounty and the environmental degradation which is fouling the ocean and sky all the way to the Antarctic.

On visits to Santiago twenty years ago we were enchanted by the European ambiance of the downtown streets adjoining Santa Lucia hill, which had first been settled by Pedro de Valdivia in the 16th century. The maids in our small hotel polished the brass daily and shined the floors by dancing around on waxy rags. When we visited there more recently the red Victorian plush was bright, the brass and wood still gleamed, but the downtown had succumbed to car and bus exhaust.

It was hardly possible to breathe in the center of the hemisphere's second most polluted city, so we fled to the slightly clearer sky of Providencia, the close-by consumer paradise where private companies were buying up condominiums in new apartment towers and outfitting them for foreigners like us. From the terrace of our stylish quarters we could see into similar apartments which held puffy foam sofas, glass tables and flashy prints identical to our own. By the time we made our next visit an even taller structure was rising across the narrow street, on which crews noisily kept pouring ever-higher cement slabs under arc lights all night long.

The avenue hummed with activity. On the lovely side streets some of the trees and elegant town houses were giving way to more towers, each with its own shopping arcade. Some emporiums were unattached, like a ramped Guggenheimian edifice labeled "The Snail". In local subway stations a network of escalators, corridors and atriums led travelers past underground and above-ground shops and services. On almost every block money changers waited behind glass.

We bought some goods and looked at price tags on others, conscious all the while that a pocket full of dollars distorted the true picture. Food and wine: modest. Jeans, shoes, children's clothes, haircut: expensive. Books: very expensive. Our own short street was a center for modish home decor, most of it imported (but friends assured us that domestic manufacture of a wide variety of consumer goods is now reviving).

Browsers and merchandise seemed plentiful, while actual buyers seemed few, making us wonder if the stylish clerks and owners could make a living. But the sidewalk entrepreneurs who appeared each morning to stake out a tiny spot on the pavement in front of shops and subway stations, spreading their cloths for hair ornaments, greeting cards, flowers, toys, clothes hangers, purses, home remedies, shoes or sunglasses, were doing a brisk business. (How different from the empty shelves and well-off women of the 1970s, desperate to buy something, anything.)

In the evenings, when a Mercedes or Toyota pulled up on the street of singles bars, a woman with an infant would emerge from the shadows to peddle holy pictures. At traffic lights on the bridges leading into Providencia small children who should have been in school dodged cars to hawk candy in the clogged traffic. Aggressive boys dogged the steps of guests emerging from a neighborhood hotel. Downtown and suburban streets were divided into small territories, each presided over by an elderly man who fed the parking meter and expected a few pennies for his efforts.

The growth of wealth and inequality has brought more crime. Those who miss the military express nostalgia for the tough way the military had handled "delinquents," while the government, its supporters, and even some of its critics seek more humane solutions.

right: Young and old Providencia Avenue peddlers sell their own crafts or whatever small household and personal items they can buy cheaply and sell at a small markup.

The Question of Truth and Justice

BARTOLO CURINIR: Seventeen years of our lives were marked by fire and pain. It's as if he died yesterday. We ask ourselves what mistakes we made to cause us to pay with the life of our son.

On October 5th, 1973, at 1:20 in the morning soldiers took away 22 year-old student Nelson Curinír. On November 27th, 1990, after an obsessive search by his parents, Zoila Lincoleo and Bartolo Curinír, Nelson became the only one of 75 disappeared persons from Temuco whose body was found. The search consumed them. Yellowing newspaper clippings, a stack of color photographs of Nelson's funeral, a university mural honoring Nelson, and a large portrait that is like a shrine dominate their lives. Over and over they relate his high academic achievements and the story of their search.

Zoila remembers the time the mayor pretended that the Air Force would release her son from custody that very afternoon, although he knew that Nelson was already dead. At first she searched alone because Bartolo was working as a teacher and other people were too frightened. As more mothers gained courage, a support group grew. Zoila appealed to lawyers and the courts. With their living children, friends and relatives, she and Bartolo even dug up riverbanks where the military had brought their pleading victims each night, and where neighbors had secretly buried corpses that had been dashed upon the rocks, and body parts carried home by dogs.

Nelson was discovered because Aylwin's election helped some people find their voices. A woman who had seen his photo in an exhibit led the family to a gravedigger who had buried a fellow without a name in somebody else's grave. Museum anthropologists identified the skull with the bullet holes from the New Imperial cemetery as Nelson's. Zoila picked up the mouldering shreds of clothing to see if they still held something of her son.

David Becker, a German psychologist who had been working with torture victims since 1983, estimated that there were 40,000 victims of "extreme traumatization" (a term first used about the holocaust) and about 200,000, if one included victims' families.

DAVID BECKER: Chile is the only dictatorship to have had human rights groups from the beginning. It was not possible to stop repression but it was possible to help some of its victims. For many years people talked of the need to stop torture, but not of its consequences for the victims and society as a whole. There has been a change in the public perception of what happened, but I don't believe the public really understands it. The first stage: Nothing happened! The second stage: It happened, but only to those who deserved it. The basic ethics of the society have been severely damaged, and the consequences will be with us for many years. It's a complicated task to repair both the victims and the social fabric.

Now the need is even greater, not less. For years it was risky to appear at our door. Silent people, whose suffering was private, are now talking. A torture victim has impossible choices: He defends his life, but hands over all that has made his life worthwhile. He defends what is dear to him, but betrays his right to live, his family. He must make a choice, and whatever he does is wrong. I believe almost everybody is forced to talk; the art is not to reveal anything important.

When you come home to your family, you cannot speak. You do not feel like a hero returning from battle; you feel destroyed, wanting to die but not having the strength to kill yourself. The objective of torture is to inflict humiliation, not to get information. Victims often feel guilt similar to that of rape victims: they must have done something to bring it on. Almost all women victims were sexually abused, many without even the pretense of interrogation. We see more women, but men are beginning to accept their right to ask for help.

In Argentina they punished the military and people said, "It's between victim and perpetrator; nothing to do with us." At Nuremberg high Nazis were punished and people said, "It's over. Nothing to do with us." But, unlike the German army, Chile's army remains intact and strong. And unlike the victims of the Nazis, most of whom fled or perished, Chilean victims remain among us. All of society must come to terms with what the torturers did to their victims.

left: Bartolo Curinír visits the grave of his son. The temporary marker reads, "Nelson Vladimir Curinír Lincoleo. Born: 30 September 1951. Disappeared: 5 October 1973. Died: 13 October 1973. Found: 27 November 1990. There is no greater love than giving your life for your friends."

Ada Pinto grew up in the small town of Huelquen, amid the vineyards and orchards of Chile's central valley. She married a local farmhand, Hugo Vidál Arenas, and they settled a few steps away in the idyllic village of El Escoriál, where she still lives with two sons and a vicious dog.

On October 3rd, 1973, when Ada was 26 years-old and her husband was 27, soldiers in blackface burst into their isolated stucco cottage in the middle of the night and dragged him off. Ada bundled up the babies and fled to her brother's house, where she saw from the road that the red military truck had arrived before her and was taking away both of her brothers. The older brother was married, with one child. The younger one was single and illiterate. None of them had been involved in politics.

Only women, children and older men remained in the tiny settlement that night. Soldiers herded 14 young peasants—barefoot, blindfolded, with hands tied—to the top of the harsh Chada hills in the dark, where they were tormented, forced to fight each other, then murdered and their corpses flung into a gully.

All this was seen at dawn by a peasant who had been asleep on the mountain but was too frightened to tell anybody until bodies and miscellaneous body parts were discovered. The news spread and the families rushed to the mountain, but the military had already posted guards to keep them away and shipped the remains to the Medical-Legal Institute—a euphemism for the Santiago morgue.

The women traveled to the Institute carrying coffins in which to bring their loved ones home but officials turned them away, claiming they had no knowledge of any bodies. For 17 years mothers and wives continued to knock at the morgue door and press authorities for information. They never got an answer.

Everybody in Huelquen had known Ada and the others all their lives, but for a long time nobody came near them or their children. Without wages, without help, without a husband, Ada was destitute. The only work she could find was as a temporary fruit picker. Her sons had to leave school as soon as they were old enough for a job.

Encouragement came mainly from the church Vicariate of Solidarity, which pressed for investigation of the disappearances and helped organize support groups among the families. In 1990 the new government appointed a special investigator who determined that the Institute still held the men in its refrigerators. In 1991, after 17 years of denying everything, morgue officials turned over the remains.

Ada, a beautiful and graceful woman, has never remarried, and she continues to live in the red stucco farmhouse. The vicious dog whose presence outside the door allayed some of her fears during the worst years now lies semi-retired and chained in the garden. It is a lonely life, but she has never considered leaving the only home she has ever known.

On the steep, parched Chada hills a sparse cover of scrub, thistles and gnarled shrubs offers little protection from the glaring sun. A single cross under a tree marks the spot where the bodies were found. Watered by rains that rush through the gully in spring-time, fertilized by the blood of the victims, that tree has grown larger and greener than any other on the inhospitable summit.

At the time the peasants of El Escoriál were finally being interred near their ancestors in the Huelquén cemetery, the massive report of the Commission on Truth and Reconciliation was delivered to President Aylwin by 81 year-old Raul Rettig, who had headed the nine member group in its study of some 2,500 crimes against humanity which had ended in death. Aylwin said, "I will risk speaking for the entire nation and ask the families of the victims for forgiveness . . . I ask solemnly that the Armed Forces and all those who were part of these excesses . . . acknowledge by some gesture the grief they have caused."

While the Air Force expressed some regret, it warned against living in the past. A group of retired generals said the report "muddled the state of affairs." The Navy claimed its own participation had been strictly professional and urged "this be our last discussion of the matter." General Pinochet, still Army chief, accused the commission of being biased, since some of its members had been victims.

But the Bishops talked of "the miscarriage of justice and the failure of public authorities," begging, "For the love of God, if anyone has information [on hidden graves] that person is obliged to share it."

The corpses of more than 70 ordinary peasants missing since the days of the coup have been discovered so far in the district of Paine, which includes Huelquén. Pinochet's amnesty law, forgiving all crimes committed from 1973 to 1978, makes it unlikely that anyone will be punished for those crimes, or any others. He still heads the army, which he threatens to unleash at the first signs of justice.

right: Ada and Alicia (whose 18 year-old brother was the youngest peasant killed that night) climb the hill to visit the place, now marked by a single cross, where soldiers threw the corpses.

right: Huelquén Cemetery, 1991. The families of the Escoriál victims come often to cover the common grave with flowers which they grow. May is a time for chrysanthamums.

The 1990s in Chile appear to be the end of the line for rule by bayonet, and an end as well to the emblem of the hammer and sickle. The early years of the decade have been marked by an orderly transition from dictatorship to democracy, but the future is by no means certain.

Our first thank-yous are for two of our own children. A teenage Judy met us in Chile in 1972 at the end of her overland journey of self-discovery. She helped with interviews and translations, and her sunny presence charmed people into trusting us. Now a professor of journalism, she is also our invaluable editor.

Ian also grew up by wandering through South America, worrying his parents when he traversed Chile during the dictatorship. When he returned there with us in 1989, his experience as a student editor and newspaper reporter, and his ease in the Spanish vernacular, made him the best kind of companion.

The first Chilean who offered to help us was Mario Planet, Dean of the Journalism School of the University of Chile, who came to our home in Massachusetts when he fled after the coup. Mario died on the other side of the Andes, while waiting until it was safe to live in his own country again.

We thank the following people—wherever they are now—for helping during the original journeys: Robin Leaver, Juan Rojo de la Rosa, Luís Fernandez Velasco, Miguel Angel Sanchez, Andrés Gacitua, Enrique Astorga, Andrés Rojas-Wainer, Santiago Bell, Eduardo Alarcón, Alberto Vega, Francisca Montes, Mishy Lesser, Judith Camus, Francisco Millán Silva, and Ciro Hermosillo. Among the bittersweet memories of those days is eating canneloni at Emilio's with Frank Teruggi, one of two young North Americans murdered by the junta.

Manuel and Frieda Agosín were generous and gracious many years ago, and remain the same today.

When we planned our return to Chile we got assistance, advice, names of contacts and encouragement from Patricia Fagen, Cristián Orrego, Cynthia Campusano, Federico Garcia Morales, Richard Fagen, Isabel Letelier, Coty Silva, Joe Eldredge, Lydia Sargent and Michael Albert.

Marjorie Agosín helped launch the companion exhibition to this volume on its national tour by arranging its opening at the Wellesley College Museum, where Kate Phelps' enthusiasm helped it succeed.

We must mention some of the individuals who went out of their way for us in Chile more recently. In Santiago: Luís Hernán Muñoz, Pedro Reyes of the National Peasant Union, Maria Angélica Kotliarenko and her assistants Ana Maria Cabello and Maria Mateluna, Moisés Labraña and Luís Suarez of the Miners' Union, Mario Gonzalez and Juan Vergara of the Textile Union, Maria Eugenia, Carlos Furche, and Mary Sue Smiaroski, who faithfully kept us informed on human rights issues.

In Temuco: Dr. Mary Sue Lowry, David Lowry, Victoria and Guillermo, Ximena Rios, and Nelson Lira. In and near Talca: Orlando Avendaño and his daughter Victoria, Marina Ramirez and Juan Plaza Ponce. We want to single out two human rights activists, Sonia Bravo in Concepción and Ruby Weitzel at the Vicariate of Solidarity in Santiago, not only for the assistance they gave us but for what they do in daily life.

For help in producing the book we are especially indebted to Martin Beveridge, as well as Ron Creamer and Jodi Slater, and Bob Adelman and Peter Miller.

Most of all, we are grateful to the Chileans you have seen in this book, and the many others who welcomed us into their lives and told us their stories.

Any institution or organization interested in learning more about the touring exhibition may write to the publisher at the address on the copyright page.